Testimonials

Beautifully written and deeply relatable. Susan is an amazing storyteller who gets to the heart and gives you pause to think about yourself and your own identity. *'Paused* reminds us that we are not our titles or our roles; we are more. It's a book that meets you wherever you are in your own becoming.

—**Nettie Nitzberg**, MEd
Coauthor of *Arrive, Drive, and Thrive*

Reading *'Paused* feels like a conversation with a wise friend—compassionate, candid, and deeply human. Susan Miele shows that even when certainty disappears, we can still find meaning and begin again.

—**Jami M. Debrango-Palumbo**
President, Strength in Heels

'PAUSED.

Susan A. Miele, PhD

'PAUSED.

Redefining Identity When Our Story No Longer Holds Us

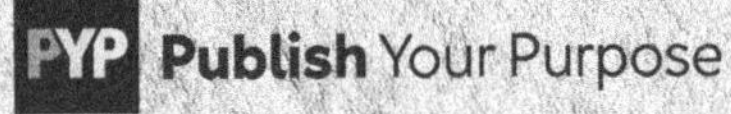

Publish Your Purpose
141 Weston Street, #155
Hartford, CT, 06141

Ordering Information: Quantity sales and special discounts are available on quantity purchases by corporations, associations, and others. For details, contact the author at susanannmiele@gmail.com.

Edited by: Lily Capstick
Cover design by: Mark Pate
Typeset by: Medlar Publishing Solutions Pvt Ltd., India

ISBN: 979-8-88797-232-9 (hardcover)
ISBN: 979-8-88797-233-6 (paperback)
ISBN: 979-8-88797-234-3 (ebook)

Library of Congress Control Number: 2026903252
First edition, May 2026

Publish Your Purpose is a hybrid publisher of nonfiction books. Our mission is to elevate the voices often excluded from traditional publishing. We intentionally seek out authors and storytellers with diverse backgrounds, life experiences, and unique perspectives to publish books that will make an impact in the world. Do you have a book idea you would like us to consider publishing? Please visit PublishYourPurpose.com for more information.

For Ken and Allison.
In all my many selves,
you were my constant—my home.

Thank you for your love, always.

To have broken through the surface of stone,
to live, to feel exposed to the madness
of the vast, eternal sky.
—Julio Noboa Polanco, *Identity*

Table of Contents

Introduction

Kaleidoscope

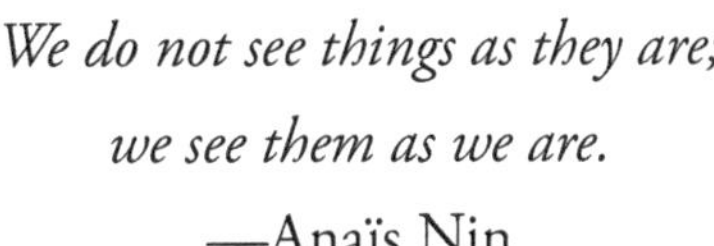

We do not see things as they are;
we see them as we are.
—Anaïs Nin

The lighting was dim, yet it could not mute the disorienting impact of the many reflections staring back at me from the kaleidoscope of mirrors in the hotel bathroom. Multiple likenesses of me sobbing, my shoulders shaking, as I tried to catch my breath on what should have been an ordinary Tuesday. I barely recognized the woman staring back at me from the dozen fragmented reflections.

I had just picked myself up from the floor, splashing water on my face in a hopeless attempt to regain composure. I was frantic. What was happening to me? Minutes earlier, I had been presenting a routine update to my colleagues when my boss asked a question about the data. I froze as I struggled to find the right words or any words at all. I couldn't. I was paralyzed. It seemed as if I were mentally unraveling. I burst into tears and fled to the nearest bathroom.

For months, I had been losing my train of thought mid-sentence. I was forgetful, irritable, and frequently irrational. But this was next level. Was I having a nervous breakdown? What else could explain hiding in a public bathroom, hysterical? My mind and heart were racing.

This was the last straw. I had to do something. My performance at work was suffering. My marriage was holding on by a thread. I was self-medicating with alcohol as I tried to manage a dizzying collection of debilitating symptoms.

Time passed slowly in the hotel bathroom. I have no idea how long I was in there or where I went when I left. The hours between my breakdown and making a cup of tea in the office kitchen the next morning were blurry, but one thing was clear: I would quit my job, immediately. I was desperate and could not see another way forward.

Shame and humiliation overwhelmed me as I stood clutching my tea so tightly, I thought the mug might break into pieces. I was vibrating with nervous energy. I was on my way to see my boss to submit my resignation. The two-minute walk to his office seemed like an eternity. I knocked tentatively on his door. As he waved me in to sit down, the embarrassment of the previous day rose in my cheeks, and my eyes filled with tears. It was so quiet, I nearly jumped when the chair creaked beneath me.

I took a deep breath, collected myself, and shared my decision with him. I offered little explanation. My performance was concerning. The stress was escalating, and my memory loss was worrisome, but I didn't elaborate. I reduced the months of cognitive decline, irrational behavior, and poor judgment down to four small words: I need a break.

I don't remember if he tried to talk me out of my decision or not, but the surprise, quickly replaced by relief on his face, was obvious.

I gave four weeks' notice. I did not have a plan. I would step into the unknown, unstable, and unemployed. I was terrified, but more than that, I was embarrassed, ashamed. I had failed. I had ruined my career. My marriage was on life support, and my sanity was slipping away. How had I let things get this bad? What was I going to do? How could I explain?

This dismantling revealed the fragility of my identity. The story I had told myself from a young age—that professional success was the key measure of my worth—was coming apart. For decades my job defined me, carrying more weight and importance than any of my other roles, even being a mom.

I had no idea who I was without the career that had made me feel seen. How would I move forward when so much of what defined me was no longer there? I didn't know how to be if I wasn't okay. Self-reliance was as central to me as breath itself, rooted in a childhood of being unseen.

Identity is often viewed as fixed, set in adolescence, and perfected incrementally over time. I now understand it differently. It is a complex puzzle, fragile, unfinished, and continually unfolding. I began to explore how identity is constructed, dismantled, and remade through the lenses of psychology, theory, and storytelling. What began as a search for answers became a more profound exploration. A chance to meet change with curiosity, to rebuild with courage, and eventually to move forward with grace.

When identity comes apart, whether abruptly or subtly, it is an invitation to rearrange the pieces. An opportunity to choose what to carry forward, what to discard, and how to become in the aftermath.

This book begins in an unfinished space. The apostrophe at the start of *'Paused* is intentional. A signal that we are entering mid-thought, mid-story, a thought interrupted, a life already in motion when it falters. By the time I understood that something was wrong, the story I had been living was already coming apart.

My story is particular, but the questions are universal. Who are we when our identities collapse? What remains? How do we rebuild?

Chapter 1

Shattered

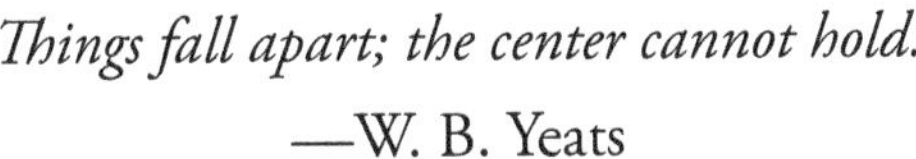

Things fall apart; the center cannot hold.
—W. B. Yeats

Six months before that fateful day in the hotel bathroom, I turned forty-two. I was at the height of my career, chief people officer (CPO) at a vibrant division of a Fortune 500 financial technology company—a position I'd held for nearly four years, two years ahead of my personal goal to reach the C-level by forty. Ken and I had been married almost eight years, and we had a beautiful five-year-old daughter named Allison, affectionately known as Alli.

My professional achievement far exceeded what I'd imagined at fourteen, when I was delivering newspapers to support myself, or at eighteen, when unloading trucks at CVS to pay my way through college. I had achieved the dream—the big job and the lifestyle that went with it—that had once seemed unattainable. We lived in a beautiful house in suburban Boston, Alli attended private school, and we had a busy social life. Ken and I thrived on hard work, managing multiple priorities, and solving challenging problems.

Years into being a wife and mother, my professional identity was vital to my sense of self. Success at work drove me. I aspired to the next C-level role, imagining myself leading HR for the entire corporation. My career had always felt certain—something I could count on.

And then, slowly, I began unraveling. Irritable, forgetful, and unable to concentrate, I would sit at my desk and stare at a simple email, abandon it midway, and wander to the office kitchen for more caffeine, hoping the fog would clear. My assistant tried to cover for me, making excuses when I was late or forgot to follow up. I blamed lack of sleep, long days, the stress of everyday life.

On one particularly trying day, a team member came to my office to give his two weeks' notice. Usually I was gracious, offering congratulations. Not this time. Tears of anger pooled in my eyes as I interrupted defensively, "How can you do this to me? You've only been here a little over a year." It was the opposite of my usual self—a hug, a warm smile, genuine happiness for someone's next move.

Stress was an easy excuse for my erratic behavior, but I *knew* it was more. I was used to managing a demanding job, frequent travel, and the pressure of keeping up with my predominantly male colleagues. What was new was a sense of dread, a growing feeling that something was wrong—*I don't feel like myself* didn't cover it. My cognitive issues were severe. I told myself to limit my drinking, sleep more, and push less. But each day grew harder.

I couldn't find the words to admit to anyone, even Ken, that I was suffering. Self-reliant since childhood, I had to figure this out on my own. But I couldn't. My symptoms accelerated. My anxiety increased as my performance at work worsened. Things at home deteriorated as I pretended to be okay.

Doctor after doctor dismissed me with stress-related diagnoses and prescriptions for anti-anxiety or antidepressant medication. My despair grew. My judgment faltered. Normally decisive, I became hesitant, frustrating my team and stalling projects.

A seismic storm was brewing. My solution was to avoid it or, worse, self-medicate with alcohol. I tossed prescriptions into the trash, drank too much, and feigned working late to avoid Ken's escalating concern. It wasn't just Ken I was avoiding. It was myself. I'd crawl into bed after the house was dark, hoping the next day would be better. It rarely was. Alcohol only deepened my downward spiral.

My declining physical and mental health became a secret that I kept even from those closest to me. Only those with a front-row seat to my collapse could see its full extent. This included my best friend Mary, who, after thirty years of friendship, could read me better than anyone. But I still couldn't say aloud that I was struggling. She didn't need my confession. She knew.

One afternoon, shortly before the hotel meltdown, we sat in my kitchen sharing a bottle of wine. She got right to the point, fearing not just the loss of my job but of Ken. If I didn't do something, she worried he might leave and take Allison with him.

Her words hit like a blow. I brushed them off, but inside they rattled me. She had named the thing I hadn't dared to think, let alone speak. Now it was real.

When the moment came—on the cold tile floor of the hotel bathroom—Mary's words returned, sharp and inescapable. I knew what I had to do.

As my last day approached, the enormity of my resignation choked me. Packing my office and saying goodbyes brought no clarity, only grief. I was walking away from a career I loved and had worked so hard to achieve, leaving a version of myself behind. I exhaled, wiped my tears, turned, and walked to my car, clinging to a shred of hope that this was the right decision, not just a desperate one.

But the fog didn't lift. Anxiety, fatigue, and apathy consumed me. The familiar labels of stress, burnout, depression—the ones doctors kept insisting on—still didn't capture the truth of my experience. They urged rest, self-care. I tried. I gave up gluten and dairy, drank green drinks, went to heated yoga daily, and put any thoughts of returning to work aside. I called it an extended sabbatical, even if that wasn't a thing in 2005. Yet my symptoms continued, undiagnosed and nearly unbearable.

Weeks later, I stood at the kitchen counter, knife in hand, staring out the window, a pile of neatly chopped vegetables before me. Allison burst through the garage door into the kitchen, her curly hair in disarray after a long day of kindergarten, her bright blue eyes shining with wonder. She skidded to a stop in front of me, gasping.

My hands were trembling from fatigue as I set the knife down, the sharp smell of red onions lingering in the air while her voice filled the kitchen.

"Momma, did you do this?" she asked, eyeing the colorful piles suspiciously.

"Yes, honey, I did." She whirled around, calling for Ken to hurry, then pointed at the counter and shouted with glee, "Daddy, Momma DID this!"

Her genuine disbelief at seeing me do something as ordinary as cutting vegetables was a small preview of an uncomfortable truth. I glanced at Ken, his mouth curving into the faintest of smiles, a look caught between surprise and worry. Our eyes met for a second, an unspoken acknowledgment passing between us before Alli spun away, her laughter echoing down the hall. She did not recognize this version of me, and neither did I.

If I was home for dinner, I typically raced through the door late, BlackBerry in hand, still tethered to the office. Now, in the absence of my work, I wasn't just unmoored. I had no idea who I was. And my delightful six-year-old had just called me out in her loud, cheerful voice, as if it were a joke.

I laughed nervously, wondering what was fun about the slow erosion of my identity. Stepping away from my job seemed like the only answer. But in reality, without my career, who was I? That day in the kitchen was only one of many filled with self-doubt, disorienting in its unfamiliarity. At first, the time away felt temporary. A brief pause, a break from the relentless pace I was used to before things would return to normal. Except nothing was normal anymore.

I had spent years not just defined by my job but by my meticulously organized schedule. I was up most days before 5 a.m., off to the gym for a spin or Pilates class, and at my desk by 7:30 a.m. Then came back-to-back meetings, deadlines, or running to catch a flight—days filled with urgency, purpose, and people relying on me. Now, there was only open space, an expanse of unstructured time. No one needed a report by noon, no emails demanded immediate attention, and no conference calls consumed my morning.

I was aimless and purposeless. I filled my time in small bits and pieces. A walk here, an errand there. Each attempt to create structure felt flimsy and artificial. The silence that replaced my old routine was deafening. And in that silence, my worries persisted. When would I feel better? Had I made a mistake? How and where would I find meaning again? Days turned into weeks as I wrestled with the loss of my professional identity, all while battling a relentless roller coaster of confusing symptoms.

I hadn't just abandoned my career. I had abandoned the version of myself I presented to the world. My new normal felt surreal and tentative. From the outside, I looked like a suburban, full-time mom or someone with a flexible schedule. Inside, I was churning with discomfort.

Early-morning yoga and Starbucks replaced my pre-dawn commute to the city. A book or newspaper stood in for my laptop, and my BlackBerry, once an appendage, now lay buried in my tote bag. Perhaps I should have felt liberated. It was the first time since I was fourteen that I didn't have a job.

Instead, I sat paralyzed, drinking my morning tea, watching the world move forward while I stayed still. I had felt important at work, but now no one seemed to notice me. I was disappearing, no longer relevant in the world I had worked so hard to belong to. It was easier for colleagues, friends, and even me to believe I had simply collapsed under the stress of my job.

Then, at my annual gynecologist appointment around the time I turned forty-three, she asked when my last period was.

I didn't know. She uttered the word *menopause*. I was confused. I had a six-year-old. Didn't menopause only happen to much older women?

It turned out that I am one of 12 percent of women globally who reach menopause before forty-five. It was actually perimenopause, the dramatic hormone fluctuation in the days and months leading up to a woman's last menstrual cycle, that had wreaked havoc on me. Something I didn't even know had a name had shattered my professional identity and disrupted my career, marriage, and sanity.

For many women, perimenopause creeps in slowly over four to seven years, its symptoms subtle at first. Mine arrived abruptly and with force, concentrated almost entirely in the psychological and cognitive realm—anxiety, brain fog, irritability, insomnia, and a persistent sense that I was losing control of my mind. Until this appointment—months after my resignation—the word *menopause* had never been mentioned. The assumption had always been the same: I was working too hard.

Even with this new information, I couldn't connect the dots. Only one explanation made sense to me. This unraveling was my fault. Blaming early menopause felt as absurd as blaming an alien invasion. Eventually I would understand it wasn't personal failure. I wasn't at fault for my undoing. I was unraveled by something that I had never seen coming. What happened to me happens to millions of women—too often in silence, alone, and unsupported.

Menopause isn't simply an individual issue. It's a societal and workplace issue, an identity-altering force that remains largely invisible. It is reduced to one day on the calendar when it is so much more—a biopsychosocial phenomenon reshaping identity through simultaneous biological, psychological, and social changes.

My identity had been built around my role as a successful professional. My self-worth was tied to my position and its status. For more than twenty years my career defined not just how I saw myself but how others saw me. Now the looks of worry I'd grown used to from Ken and my colleagues rippled outward—my family, friends, neighbors—each one struggling to find the right words.

Except for my dad. Blunt as ever, he stared at me aghast. "What the hell, Susan? You quit your job? Without one? You'll lose your house! Have you lost your mind?" I thought, well, yes, Dad, I think I have. But don't worry. We need to sell the house. I said nothing. The shame was suffocating.

Yet life moved on. Ken went to work, Alli went to school, and I wandered through each day with no escape, nowhere to hide. The tension at home stabilized, but my emotional disconnection remained. I increased my hours on my yoga mat, punishing myself in ninety minutes of heated power vinyasa, hoping for respite. For a time, it helped. The anxiety eased just enough for me to feel faint flickers of my old self.

It was enough for us to move forward. We sold our house to downsize to a less expensive community where we would enroll Alli in public school. Leaving that house was almost as hard as leaving my job. It wasn't just walls and a roof. It was part of us. Walking away felt like closing the door on another unfinished chapter.

Thankfully, even on the darkest days, Ken's love and commitment never wavered. Even at his angriest, even at wit's end, even if he considered leaving—he didn't. What mattered most at this moment in time was that Ken and I were taking our next step—together. The rest we would figure out.

Oh, and I was in menopause. Somehow, that felt almost beside the point.

Except it wasn't.

Twelve days after moving into our new house, I was at the printer in my office, wearing pajama pants, Uggs, and a hoodie, when I caught a faint flicker of orange in the corner of my eye. A spark pulsed against the window glass—small, but alive. I stared, uneasy. It returned brighter, larger. My stomach tightened.

I called upstairs to Ken, who was working in the office above me. He came down, mildly annoyed, and swung open the bright red front door. He gasped.

> "The porch is on fire."
>
> He turned toward me, eyes wide. "Go get Alli!"

Adrenaline carried me up the stairs despite months of bone-deep fatigue. I woke Allison gently.

> "Honey, you need to get up. We have a fire."
>
> "Momma, what kind of fire?" she murmured, half-asleep.
>
> "I don't know."
>
> "Is it a stop, drop, and roll fire?"
>
> "I have no idea. Let's go."

Only minutes earlier I had been settling into my office to organize my materials for a consulting opportunity I had been hired for. My first attempt at work since leaving my job almost a year earlier. It lacked the prestige, pay, and responsibility of my old position, but it was something, a small step toward reclaiming a shred of my professional identity. My new outfit, shoes, and jewelry were laid out upstairs, ready for the morning. I had been too restless to sleep, a mix of excitement and anxiety humming through me. That spark in the window had barely registered.

Ken met us at the bottom of the stairs. He picked Allison up and ushered us toward the back door. I grabbed my wallet and my BlackBerry on the way—my BlackBerry, the remaining talisman that somehow felt like proof that I was still tethered to my career, to who I was before menopause. For a split second I considered what else to take, but Ken pulled me outside just as the front window shattered and smoke poured in.

We stumbled into the backyard, the cold night air a shock. Reality hit—this was our brand-new house, our supposed fresh start. I whispered to myself, *It's going to be okay*, but Ken knew otherwise.

He said quietly, "The fire is in the wall. It's not on the porch."

In denial, I pretended not to hear him as we rounded to the front of the house. The entire façade was ablaze. This was not a minor inconvenience. Our house was burning down before our eyes.

Fire trucks arrived. My brother-in-law, an off-duty firefighter, pulled up as I stood on the verge of hysteria. Allison was taken in by the only other family on the street, safe inside with hot chocolate, her favorite angel-embroidered nightgown hidden under a borrowed sweatshirt.

My brother-in-law spoke quietly with the firefighters before approaching me. "This is going to be okay," I said aloud, as if willing it true. He shook his head, slowly, and sadly, as he said, "No, it isn't, Susan. You won't be going back into that house."

"What?" I choked. "That can't be. Everything we own is in there."

As if on cue, the garage roof collapsed, igniting both our cars. I fell to my knees on the grass, slowly pulling myself to stand just as Allison came running from the neighbor's house, swallowed up by an oversized Boston Bruins sweatshirt that came down to her ankles.

A firefighter approached. "Any pets or anything that needs rescuing?"

Anything other than everything we own? I screamed silently—my wedding rings, Allison's baby clothes, her artwork, our family Christmas ornaments, our collection of pottery. I shook my head. "No pets."

Allison piped up, "MY BIKE! Can you get my bike?" Her new birthday present sat just inside the garage. The firefighter nodded gently, though we both knew it was probably already lost.

Needless to say, I didn't start that consulting position the next morning. My carefully chosen outfit, my folder of directions, my symbolic reentry into a lesser version of my former career—all of it was gone in a matter of hours.

I was grateful we were safe, but gratitude didn't erase the truth. Menopause had already taken my career. Now the fire had taken everything else. Another little piece of me died that night—not just in the flames, but in the loss of the things that held our memories, our stories, and the fragile sense of who I believed I still was.

We returned to the house the next day. The smoke had cleared, and the damage was irreparable. Barely anything was recognizable, a pile of burnt timber and debris. What remained would eventually be boarded up and condemned, declared uninhabitable, a complete loss. I, too, was a complete loss. I had never felt so raw, so vulnerable. I was standing there dazed, gazing at the wreckage dressed in a friend's clothes, even her *underwear.*

It was as if we were holding a wake for the house that morning. Family and friends arrived to inspect the damage and pay their condolences. Ken and I stood side by side at the bottom of the steps, a receiving line of sorts, as people approached, hugging us, shaking their heads in disbelief at the wreckage, and trying to console us with well-meaning sentiments:

> *It could have been so much worse.*
>
> *It's just stuff.*
>
> *You could have died.*

We were stunned and exhausted as we nodded and wondered what the hell we were going to do next. I could barely speak as I tried to grasp the extent of my undoing. I didn't even own a pair of *underwear.* The story that I had been living inside since my resignation, where the house, possessions, and the new neighborhood were visible proof that despite my downfall, I was okay, was no longer psychologically sustainable. Instead, a refrain played in my head like a soundtrack on repeat. *All that remains is me. Everything else is gone.*

There were no remaining external markers of my identity to hold onto. What was left of my internal scaffolding collapsed, the one built around the illusion of control and safety. The new house and the work of moving had been holding me up as I struggled to manage my menopause symptoms and regain my sense of self.

Now it, too, was gone, replaced with disorienting grief and fear. I had written my story of professional and personal success, and once I had achieved it, I became the story. I had no story now. And without a story, I had no meaning. My narrative identity—the internalized story I had constructed to give my life purpose and cohesion—had been erased. Not by choice, not because I had decided it was time to craft another story, but by events that left me undone. I was now a character without a plot.

The fire happened on Easter weekend. Amid condolences, Allison received half a dozen Easter baskets, each overflowing with candy and stuffed bunnies. We had no house, no clothes, no cars, but so many stuffed bunnies. The absurdity rattled me.

In the weeks that followed, I moved through the world in a daze. Practically, there was much to do—find temporary housing, return Allison to school, and tackle insurance paperwork that demanded I tally every sock and towel we had owned. I wanted to linger in my despair and wallow in grief, yet the insurance company demanded spreadsheets. One day, overwhelmed by the banality of listing socks, I slammed the laptop shut, cursing at the plastic plants in our bland temporary apartment.

Allison wrapped her arms around me. "What's the matter, Momma? Don't you like it here?"

> "It's not that, honey. It's just that this isn't home."
>
> Her face lit up. "But Momma, don't be sad—we have a pool!"

Until perimenopause, I had never met a challenge I couldn't overcome. Now my young daughter was comforting me. It was humbling and heartbreaking.

I drifted through the weeks after the fire in a liminal space. Liminality is an experience of in-betweenness. It is the metaphorical hallway where one door closes behind you and the new one has yet to open. There is no certainty in this hallway, no knowing what is behind that next door, only possibilities.

At first, I told myself this was an intermission, a break before normalcy returned. But as the weeks stretched on, I began to glimpse the truth. Nothing would return to how it was. The past was gone, the present fragile, the future unknown.

In less than a year, two pillars of my identity had collapsed. My professional self, the foundation of my worth, and our home, the visible proof of success. The dismantling begun by menopause was now complete, demolished by fire. The question echoed: *When everything that defined you is gone, what remains?*

Even my reflection felt like a stranger. My body had become unfamiliar as menopause and trauma completed their takeover. I was thin to the point of frailty, weighing less than 120 pounds, my hair falling out, my diet reduced to green tea and wine.

The cumulative impact of menopausal symptoms and stress felt insurmountable.

One morning, harsh light deepened the shadows under my eyes as I leaned over the sink. The mirror didn't lie. It showed a woman whose confidence and spark had vanished. More than my looks, it was my sense of self that I no longer recognized.

And yet, I couldn't stay lost forever.

No matter what the mirror said, somewhere inside, I still existed.

Months blurred as we battled insurance claims for the total loss of our house, cars, and possessions. The builder refused to work with us, fearing a lawsuit we never filed. I wanted to scream—*this is so unfair*. Instead, I buried my feelings, intellectualized them, and pressed on. There were spreadsheets to complete, cabinets and paint to choose, and endless lists needed to replace a decade of belongings.

Ken moved into get-it-done mode, while Allison embraced her celebrity status as the new girl in town whose house had burned down. Before the fire, she had one American Girl doll. After, she had three. She kept me grounded, urging in her small but insistent voice, "Don't be sad, Momma. Everything is okay." Her spirit and energy propelled me forward when dread threatened to consume me.

Still, I wasn't strong or hopeful. I was existing, not emerging—stuck in liminality. Searching for meaning would come later. For now, there were socks to count, towels to list. Small, sometimes absurd steps that I pretended were part of healing.

By fall, the day arrived to demolish what remained of the house. We stood together as the backhoe pushed the walls inward, the remains of ordinary household items flashing briefly in the rubble before vanishing. Allison climbed into the cab, tugging levers with delight. I backed up to the same spot I had stood the night of the fire and watched as the leg of our dining room table—curved, hand-painted with bright flowers—spun through the air, beautiful for a fleeting second before disappearing for good.

It wasn't just the house being demolished. It was the last fragile pieces of who I had been.

The foundation, however, remained. From it, a new house would rise. The structure would look familiar, but nothing inside would be the same. And neither would I.

Around that time, the consulting opportunity that had vanished with the fire returned. The email was simple. *Are you still interested?* I paused before responding, surprised to feel something stir. Maybe even readiness.

Chapter 2

Unseen, Not Unloved

Being seen is the most basic of human needs.
—Susan Harter

I don't remember where I was when President John F. Kennedy was shot. I was thirteen months old. My mother never remembered either.

She frequently told the story about how she had learned the terrible news from the milkman. It was early afternoon on a cloudy, cool November day in Boston when the milkman pulled up to the back door of our small Somerville house. Bottles clinked in their wire frame, his usual cheerful demeanor noticeably off.

"The president's been shot," he said.

No greeting. No small talk. Just the news.

My mother was five months pregnant with my younger sister, Carol. My dad and older sister, Mary, who was three and a half, were playing checkers in the family room, a dark wood-paneled room with shag carpeting that we grew up calling the den. My mom stood for a moment alone in the kitchen in shock, holding her belly with one hand and the door with the other, trying to understand what she had just heard. She had worked on Kennedy's presidential campaign and had the chance to meet him. As an Irish Catholic in Boston, she was a devoted and unwavering Democrat.

She called my dad to turn on the television as she hurried into the family room.

The last time I remember her telling this story was on Thanksgiving Day in 2013, the fiftieth anniversary of Kennedy's assassination. I was fifty-one. A guest had asked her, "Where were you when President Kennedy was shot, Elizabeth?"

As she recounted the story, I knew every detail by heart, including the answer to the question I occasionally lobbed at her to see if the answer might change, knowing it wouldn't: "Where was I, Mom?" Her reply was always the same—not dramatic, just factual: "I don't know where you were. You were probably in that playpen thing." But she didn't know where I was, not at the time, and not in the fifty years since she had been telling this story.

I imagined myself in the corner of the dim family room, contained in a cheap plastic playpen, watching the world respond to history without noticing I was there. It may seem like a small detail, but it wasn't to me. Even in my mom's story of an unforgettable day, I was invisible, and I wasn't even two.

I often wondered why she didn't pretend to know where I was. I never had the courage to ask. Maybe I feared the answer. Or perhaps I already knew it. This was the beginning of my being unseen, a truth that would quietly shape who I became. It was the first layer in the foundation of an identity built as much from absence as from presence.

We don't remember our earliest stories, but they remember us. Developmental psychologists Robyn Fivush and Marshall Duke have shown that the stories our families tell—and the ones they leave untold—form a blueprint for our sense of self. It doesn't matter if we were too young to recall the event. The way others remember us, speak about us, or forget to speak of us becomes a pattern that writes itself into our internal scripts.[1]

The story of the day President Kennedy was assassinated was told more times than I can count. Over the years, its message etched itself into me as deeply as the event itself is etched into history. I was not part of the story. I was not remembered. I was not seen.

It wasn't because of malice or neglect in the traditional sense. I simply wasn't part of the emotional focus. The omission was repeated so casually it never seemed worth noting. Yet, it left a blank space in the family's picture of that day. A gap where I should have been. I felt its weight long before I knew how to speak.

This early narrative of being unseen became more than a missing detail in my life story. It became the story.

Foundational to this narrative is what psychologist Jonice Webb calls childhood emotional neglect (CEN).[2] I never experienced abuse or cruelty. I experienced absence. A heartbreaking lack of being seen or understood. An absence that shaped my development from childhood through adolescence.

---

[1] Marshall P. Duke et al., "Knowledge of Family History as a Clinically Useful Index of Psychological Well-Being and Prognosis: A Brief Report," *Psychotherapy: Theory, Research, Practice, Training* 45, no. 2 (2008): 268.

[2] Jonice Webb, *Running on Empty: Overcome Your Childhood Emotional Neglect* (Morgan James Publishing, 2012).

I was in fourth grade when I failed the school hearing test. I had just turned nine. I didn't raise my hand when the other kids did. I didn't know how a hearing test worked. It was the first time my hearing had ever been checked, but I knew something was off. Then it was confirmed. The woman administering the test wrote a bold "F" next to my name on the clipboard. I could see it clearly from where I stood. My eyesight was excellent.

At nine, I was already well on my way to academic overachievement. A year earlier, I had won the third-grade spelling bee and recited all fifty states and their capitals without a single mistake. My prize for this dual feat was a gigantic stuffed frog, proudly displayed on my bed like a trophy. I was not a child who failed academically. When I didn't raise my hand at the correct times during the hearing test, I assumed it was a mistake. It never occurred to me that I couldn't hear. I must have misunderstood the instructions.

That night at dinner, which was always promptly at 5:30 p.m., the five of us gathered around the small round table in our crowded kitchen. "I failed the hearing test today," I said anxiously. I expected concern, maybe even disappointment. But my mother simply replied, flatly, "No, you didn't."

My father didn't say anything. That wasn't unusual, but on rare occasions, he would take my side, and in those moments, I felt seen, validated—even if fleeting. I stared at him, willing him to say something. Anything. He didn't.

My dad's quietness was often mistaken for care or for his unwillingness to disagree with my mother. He was a man of few words, but the truth is when he did speak, his directness could land like a blow. Sometimes careless, sometimes cruel. But that night, he let the moment pass without comment.

That was it—conversation over. No questions. No follow-up. No support.

A week later, my mother attended an adult education class taught by the same woman who had given the hearing test. My mom was with my aunt, who shared the same last name. Our families were closely intertwined; my cousins, sisters, and I all attended the same elementary school.

At the start of class, the teacher asked, "Which one of you is Susan's mother?"

"I am," my mother said.

"Oh," the teacher replied. "Susan failed the hearing test last week."

My mother was stunned. I had failed the test. Why hadn't the school contacted her? She was incredulous. I was confused the next day when she marched down to the school to "get to the bottom" of what I had already told her. Why hadn't she believed me? Instead, she insisted I see countless ear doctors for more rounds of humiliating hearing tests. I failed them all.

Months later, my prognosis was confirmed. I was completely deaf in my right ear. It was likely congenital. Nerve damage. Permanent. I was born unable to hear from that ear and no one had noticed. I was shaken, not just by the diagnosis, but by what it confirmed. My parents never saw me. Not when I was a baby. Not when I was nine. Not even when I told them something was wrong.

I was not unloved. Unseen, yes. Unloved, no.

My parents were hardworking, caring, and generous. I never doubted they were doing the best they could, yet that doesn't change the lasting impact their neglect had on me. Dr. Webb's theory describes parents like mine as well-intentioned, doing the best they can within the limits of their own upbringing.[3] Many years later, this makes sense to me. My mom and dad were children of immigrants, born in the shadow of the Great Depression. Their childhoods were shaped by scarcity and survival. I imagine emotions were a luxury my grandparents couldn't afford.

My dad's father never spoke English. A few words here and there, but he could not hold a conversation. Each morning, he would walk down our street calling out happily to my sisters and me, "Hey, Nono." Nono is what we called him. As kids, we would laugh, smile, and wave to him from our front porch as he made his way to work. We thought it was funny, that he called us Nono, not understanding that he couldn't clearly pronounce our names.

Nono came to the United States from Italy. He was a merchant marine who abandoned his ship in search of a better life. He eventually made it to Somerville to marry my grandmother. They had four sons. My dad was the oldest. My dad grew up in a house where words themselves were scarce. Feelings were definitely scarcer. My grandparents were too focused on the basics of work, food, and survival to make room for emotion. My dad carried that scarcity forward, his love expressed through his actions, his hard work, not his words. It was the only language he knew.

I am pretty sure emotions were equally rare when my mom was growing up. Her mom immigrated to Boston from Ireland.

---

[3] Webb, *Running on Empty*, 65.

Gram was born in the aftermath of the Irish potato famine. She was strong and tall, never a demonstratively warm person. Gram had an air of endurance and survival, not a cuddly grandmother vibe. Her love mainly came through her actions; she handmade beautiful clothes for us, often matching outfits stitched with precision and love. I still remember a corduroy jumper that I adored, green with front pockets. Green was my favorite color.

When we were young, we would wait for Gram out in front of our house, eyes fixed on the corner where she would appear. The moment she came into view, we would run to meet her, talking over each other to get her attention. Gram had a lovely brogue, a sharp wit, and little patience for nonsense. My mother was a lot like her, minus the brogue.

My parents carried all of this into their own lives: the values of work, endurance, and practicality. My dad spent his career working at a shipyard; my mom was a secretary. They stretched what they had to give us stability and provide for us. By most measures, I had a normal, happy childhood.

Family was all around us, and community shaped my early years. We lived in a neighborhood teeming with children. My dad's parents and his brother across the street, my aunt and her family around the corner, and Gram lived with my aunt and cousins just a few blocks away. We were raised Catholic, attended Sunday school, and made all our sacraments at a beautiful church up on the hill.

There were front steps, sidewalks, and an endless rotation of playmates on our street, which overflowed with families like ours. My parents were social and often hosted gatherings filled with laughter, food, and a houseful of relatives who were much more than occasional guests. My mother always made holidays special; Christmas mornings were magical, and birthdays were always celebrated. We took a one-week vacation every summer, usually with cousins, aunts, and uncles—modest but joyful—and I have many fond memories of those trips.

There was love. There was structure. There were traditions.

Still, something was missing. I never quite fit, often feeling like I was on the outside looking in. I generally attributed this to being the middle child.

My older sister was strong-willed and quick to argue, commanding attention simply by being the oldest. My younger sister was more needy, looking for reassurance rather than the spotlight, and as my mother's obvious favorite, she often got it.

Between them, I became the steady one. It was easier to be the calm in the storm than to compete for attention that I wasn't likely to get. Middle children often feel overlooked. They adapt out of necessity.[4] I was no exception.

My adaptability looked like competence, but underneath it was intention. I sought the path of least resistance, the role that kept the peace and cost me the least emotionally. I looked for attention through achievement, independence, and over-functioning, starting at an early age.

My emotional self-sufficiency felt like a superpower. The ability to quietly excel under the radar without much fuss. My parents' lack of attention reinforced what became the cornerstone of my identity before I turned ten—self-reliance. It wasn't just

---

[4] Catherine Salmon and Katrin Schumann, *The Secret Power of Middle Children: How Middleborns Can Harness Their Unexpected and Remarkable Abilities* (Penguin, 2012).

a coping strategy. It was who I became. Capable, independent, fine on my own.

Psychologists have long studied how these early family patterns shape our sense of self. John Bowlby's seminal work on attachment theory suggests that a child's earliest bonds form the blueprint for how they connect or don't connect to others. When emotional needs go unmet, children often develop what Bowlby calls an avoidant attachment style. They learn, often unconsciously, to suppress their needs and depend solely on themselves rather than risk being unseen or dismissed.[5]

Until I faced my own collapse from menopause and the fire, I didn't understand that identities built around emotional absence are not durable. They hold for a time until something causes them to give way.

While attachment theory explains how our earliest relationships shape emotional expectations, Dr. Webb's work narrows the focus of this experience to what isn't said, what isn't felt, and what is quietly missing in day-to-day life. CEN is the white space in a family picture—not what is visible, but what is missing.[6]

Identity is formed not only by what is present but also by what is absent. Love without belonging or visibility leaves a child lonely in ways that are hard to name. Emotional neglect doesn't erase joyful memories; it runs alongside them, stealthy but no less impactful. I wasn't mistreated, but I wasn't known. I never felt like I mattered.

---

[5] John Bowlby, "The Bowlby-Ainsworth Attachment Theory," *Behavioral and Brain Sciences* 2, no. 4 (1979): 637–38.

[6] Webb, *Running on Empty*.

Even on my birthday, I often felt lonely. My sisters were born a day apart, four years apart, and celebrated together every spring. My October birthday was quieter, smaller, lacking the same energy and excitement. I learned early that being included in an occasion wasn't the same as being part of it.

Therapists call a caregiver's ability to recognize and respond to a child's emotional needs with empathy and presence *attunement*.[7] My parents didn't lack love; they simply couldn't connect with me emotionally. They weren't attuned to my needs. Children who grow up this way, as I did, often become highly functional. They become achievers and perfectionists, performing well on the outside even as their inner world remains invisible.

In childhood, my achievements lived in my good grades. My parents frequently told me that as long as I did well in school, I would be successful. I took this quite literally, bringing home all As more often than not. I kept my needs minimal and my voice low. I frequently played the peacemaker, moderating disagreements between my sisters.

As I approached adolescence, the feeling of invisibility that had shaped my childhood identity didn't fade. It solidified. My foundation already hardened by age twelve. I was capable, independent, and reliable. This strong sense of self gave me a confidence that was deceiving, even if it appeared admirable or enviable. It was built on my understanding that needing less attention, care, or involvement made me stronger, yet echoed that feeling that I didn't really matter.

[7] Webb, *Running on Empty*, 11.

Developmental psychologist Erik Erikson described this stage, between ages six and twelve, as a time for developing competence and productivity.[8] For me, being competent and productive wasn't just a developmental milestone. It was a matter of identity. I didn't simply strive for excellence. I depended on it. My sense of self seemed solid because it left no room for uncertainty, no space for vulnerability, and no margin for failure.

By the time I entered adolescence, the stage Erikson calls *identity versus role confusion*, I wasn't searching for who I was. I already knew—or thought I did. I clung to what had worked: achievement, control, and perfection.[9] My identity was functional, polished, and unyielding. This message had been deeply internalized and had become a part of me. Be good so you can be successful. It played on a loop.

When I caught those fleeting moments of parental attention, I tried to make sure they were positive, reflecting what they needed, not necessarily what I needed. I wasn't emotionally aware enough to recognize that this drive wasn't entirely my own. I clung to believing that achievement and self-sufficiency were enough to earn love. It would take decades to fully understand how much of my sense of self had been shaped by a longing to be seen.

This was the early 1970s in Somerville, Massachusetts, a working-class city with narrow streets, triple-deckers stacked like dominoes, and a scrappy charm that could be both rough and endearing. There was always a hum of danger just beneath the surface: whispered stories about the Winter Hill boys, bookies

---

[8] Erik Erikson, *Identity: Youth and Crisis* (Norton, 1968).

[9] Erikson, *Identity: Youth and Crisis.*

at the corner store, a sense that certain lines weren't meant to be crossed.

But for me, it was simply home. A place where I learned to be tough, to trust my instincts, and to find my way.

I roamed those streets freely in my early adolescence, rarely feeling afraid. I was used to caring for myself, not just emotionally, but existentially. Independence was as essential to me as air.

And then, on the first day of seventh grade, something unexpected happened. I met my best friend, Mary.

I was twelve, awkwardly tall—almost my full adult height—nervous, sitting in a math class that felt unfamiliar in a new school that might as well have been in a different city, even though it was just a few blocks from my house.

When she took her seat beside me, I had no idea that she would profoundly change my life. From that point forward, I had a place where I belonged. Mary understood me when it felt like no one else did. Mary made me laugh, and, most importantly, she made me feel like I mattered. We were kindred spirits from the start, immediately at ease with each other and sharing a way of seeing the world. Mary took me seriously. She listened, valued my opinions, appreciated my quirks, and recognized my intelligence. Until meeting Mary, I struggled not only with feelings of not being seen or fitting in, but also with never having my *own* friend, a best friend, someone uniquely mine.

In the chaotic, crowded neighborhood we grew up in, my sisters and I were regularly unidentifiable, lost among a group of at least a dozen kids, including many of our first cousins. We were always part of a pack, playing together, chasing each other around someone's yard with a backyard hose, or sitting with legs crossed, deep into a competitive game of jacks on the sidewalk at the end of a hot day. Our friendships were all shared and mostly interchangeable; whoever was around to play *played.*

This changed when I met Mary. From that first day in seventh grade, Mary and I were inseparable. Our lives came together in a way that shaped both of us.

We started meeting most mornings before school in the dim cafeteria of the old middle school building to finish up outstanding homework and discuss the day ahead. Mary's father owned a convenience store, and she would arrive an hour or so before classes started with a cheese and pickle sandwich from the store that we would share for breakfast.

At the last bell, we would hang out in front of the school until all of the other kids had departed for home. Only then would we walk to one of our houses to spend the afternoon sharing secrets and snacks until separating for family dinner. On the weekends and holidays, we would meet up after dinner at 6:30 sharp at a designated poorly lit street corner roughly halfway between our two houses.

By thirteen, we had become part of a larger crowd, a mixed group of girls and boys who gathered at a local schoolyard or on the railroad tracks after dark. We were popular enough among this large group, spending whatever free time we could anywhere but at home. No matter the weather, you could find us somewhere in the vicinity of Somerville Avenue. Once, during a record-breaking blizzard, we spent hours wandering around, our crowded city having morphed into a snowy tundra.

It wasn't long after joining this larger group that we started experimenting with drinking and marijuana. This was Somerville in the '70s, after all, and alcohol and drugs were easy to access, even at thirteen. Luckily, we never got in serious trouble, nor did these dubious choices sway us from excelling in school or finding jobs at fourteen so we could support ourselves and save for college. I delivered newspapers early in the morning, and Mary worked behind the counter in her father's store.

Mary's friendship didn't unwind the identity I had been refining since early childhood. It helped further entrench it. I was still self-reliant, high-achieving, and circumspect.

I still believed I had to earn my place through excellence. But now, I had someone who understood me and stood beside me, sharing not just the weight of growing up but the unspoken belief that we could make it out together.

While Mary wasn't the first mirror through which I saw myself, she was the first to allow me to see a version of myself that belonged—a version that mattered.

Mary didn't just reflect me back. She saw me.

Sociologist Charles Horton Cooley called this the *looking-glass self*—the idea that we come to know who we are by seeing ourselves reflected in the eyes of others.[10] Until I met Mary, I had always felt invisible, like I had never truly been seen.

The me-against-the-world posture I had developed—my avoidant attachment style—began to soften in the presence of her steady friendship. Identity, I would come to understand, is neither fixed nor formed in isolation. It is shaped in and through our closest relationships.

---

[10] Charles Cooley, *Human Nature and the Social Order* (Scribner, 1902).

For the first time, I wasn't just surviving on self-reliance but becoming someone in connection. This relational self wasn't an obscure theory. It was unfolding in real-time, reshaping me.[11] With Mary, I began to see myself differently because she saw me differently. The self I was becoming was recognized, affirmed, and confident.

But while friendship gave me a sense of being seen, home told a different story. The expectations at home were simple: be good, stay out of trouble, and come home on time. As long as I met those conditions, there was little engagement or interest. My parents didn't know where I was most of the time and didn't ask. I was free to roam Somerville's streets, learning how to grow up on my own.

This lack of interest didn't change as I got older. It was a continuation of what had always been. By thirteen, I knew that being noticed—honestly noticed—only happened when I'd done something wrong. I'd learned to stay under the radar. I found my way, for better or for worse.

If childhood taught me to care for myself, adolescence reinforced that lesson. If I wanted something, I had to earn it without any help. And by sixteen, I was well on my way to doing so. In addition to excellent grades and a spot in the National Honor Society, I landed my first real job at the CVS store, just a mile from my house.

I was a junior in high school, and my dream of going to college and getting out of Somerville was starting to feel real.

---

[11] Judith V. Jordan, "Relational–Cultural Theory: The Power of Connection to Transform Our Lives," *The Journal of Humanistic Counseling* 56, no. 3 (2017): 228–43.

My world consisted of working as many hours as possible at CVS, maintaining high grades, and socializing with Mary and our large friend group whenever I wasn't busy with work or school.

Academics came easily to me, starting with that long-ago third-grade spelling bee. My sense of self-worth rested comfortably in the quiet certainty that I was smart. I preferred challenging assignments, was naturally curious, and found that mastering complex subjects brought me a satisfaction I couldn't find anywhere else.

The competence I developed in school transitioned naturally into early work success, and the seeds of my professional identity began to take root. At CVS, I quickly became the front-of-store supervisor, training new cashiers, counting drawers at night, and making bank deposits. Before I graduated high school, I had the keys to the store and opened it some mornings on my own.

Psychologist Susan Harter describes scholastic competence as a significant domain of self-worth in adolescence—but for me, that sense of capability extended beyond the classroom.[12] Doing well at work gave me the same validation I sought through grades. It was another way to prove I mattered.

The more capable I felt at work, the more motivated I was to prove myself. I figured out, even then, that this was the way forward: work hard, earn trust, and keep going. A future where I was respected, relied on, and no longer invisible—that's what I imagined. But first, I had to get myself to college, with limited options and, unsurprisingly, very little support at home.

---

[12] Susan Harter, *The Construction of the Self: Developmental and Sociocultural Foundations*, 2nd ed. (The Guilford Press, 2012).

College wasn't a given for most graduates of Somerville High School's class of 1980. Many of my classmates chose the military, a trade, or civil service. Others fell victim to drugs, crime, or the harder edges of Somerville's streets.

I would be the first in my immediate family to go to college and only the second in my large extended family. I had no idea how I would pull it off, but not going never occurred to me. I couldn't abandon the dream that Mary and I had held dear since seventh-grade math class.

As senior year approached, I brought it up to my parents, fully expecting the lukewarm response I received. I don't remember their exact words, but it went something like: "Sure, Susan, you can go to college—as long as you figure it out and pay for it yourself." It wasn't surprising. But it still stung. It reinforced what I had learned long ago, ever since the day I failed the hearing test in fourth grade: What I did or didn't do didn't really matter.

After that conversation with my parents, my decision on where to go to college narrowed. The only practical option was the state school that I could commute to while living at home and continuing to work at CVS. I would minimize my college debt by paying as I went, taking public transportation, and maintaining a full-time work schedule, managing my classes around my hours at CVS.

It wasn't exactly the college experience I hoped for, but I was determined to make the best of it. Mary would also commute to college and live at home for entirely different reasons. We had imagined moving away, sharing a dorm, traveling in a whole new world, but we never did realize those dreams. Nevertheless, we were heading to college that fall. We would do it our way, independent, yet deeply connected as we ventured out of Somerville, onto our next adventure.

It was 1980, the last summer before college. I walked to CVS most mornings to meet and unload the truck at 6 a.m., then stock the shelves and open the store by 9 a.m. My only stop was to grab a very large coffee from the Dunkin' Donuts next to the store. Once my shift ended, I would rush home to rest until it was time to meet Mary.

At almost eighteen, we had a new sense of freedom. Mary had a car. No more hanging around at the schoolyard or the railroad tracks. We hit the road whenever we could. Our destination—a cheap motel and even cheaper booze in a honkytonk beach town on Cape Cod or New Hampshire. We would spend the days at the beach and the nights at whatever dance club would take our fake IDs, dancing and drinking until the early morning hours, sleeping for a bit, and then repeating until we would return home exhausted and sunburned.

We pushed boundaries and took risks, adding many stories and laughs to our lifetime of memories from that particularly crazy summer. We didn't want it to end. Fall was fast approaching. Mary was attending Northeastern University, and I was headed to UMass Boston.

We hadn't been separated since seventh grade. Mary was part of how I understood who I was in so many ways. She had been there through the striving, the uncertainty, the grit. I had formed a stronger sense of self through my connection with her. Her presence affirmed me.

As that first day of college grew near, I wondered how life would change as I transitioned from the rough-and-tumble streets of Somerville to the sprawling cement landscape of UMass's downtown campus. Would the confidence and belonging I had found through this essential friendship sustain me? Or would I once again find myself alone—me against the world?

Today, this phase of adolescence is called emerging adulthood, a time to test paths before settling into life.[13] That wasn't my story. By seventeen, I had launched into adulthood, working full-time at CVS, earning a bachelor's degree at night, and paying my way, with the ever-present understanding that no one was coming to catch me if I fell.

My schedule at CVS remained essentially unchanged once college started. Instead of socializing after work, I grabbed another large Dunkin' coffee and jumped on the subway to my afternoon and evening classes; I was studying management. UMass was a commuter-only school in the 1980s, with schedules that accommodated working students like me.

These long days continued for six years, when I finally earned my bachelor's degree. Many things changed during this time, while many stayed the same. Mary was still my closest friend, but it was different now. We both had serious relationships and increased responsibility and were, practically speaking, adults.

I dated in high school, but never with much success. My first real relationship with a boy I was crazy about ended in humiliation when I learned he had been dating someone else all along. I was serious and contemplative, while high school boys were not.

---

[13] Jeffrey Jensen Arnett, "Emerging Adulthood: A Theory of Development from the Late Teens through the Twenties," *American Psychologist* 55, no. 5 (2000): 469.

I balanced my academic focus with my social life and didn't worry too much about boys, until I met Joe.

I was eighteen. He was twenty-three. He wasn't the kind of person I imagined as my first true love—older, with no college degree, more inner-city than me, and rough around the edges. But Joe made me feel special. Not the polished, capable version of me the world saw, but the real me.

With Joe, I felt safe, not because I needed protection, but because he got me. He understood my seriousness, my ambition, and, maybe most importantly, my longing to be seen. His belief in me helped me believe more deeply in myself. Joe expanded the story of who I was becoming.

But in the end, after a few years of dating, I didn't choose Joe. It was one of the hardest decisions I have ever made. My heart wanted one thing and my head another.

I had learned, been conditioned even, to contain my emotions, to solve problems with reason rather than risk the uncertainty of feeling. Vulnerability wasn't a language I understood. Choosing Joe would have meant leading with my heart, and that felt dangerous in a way I couldn't name back then.

With Joe, I feared I would remain on the outside—struggling to fit in, to belong in the broader social world, and, most of all, within my own family. The five-year age difference between Joe and me was more than just time. It was a distance in experience and choices. I was on a straight and narrow path. Joe not so much. It was more than the absence of a college degree and his rough edges. Joe didn't have a plan, spending most of his free time drinking and gambling. At only twenty-one, bridging the gap between Joe and my family's expectations felt too difficult, nearly impossible. I couldn't imagine spending the rest of my life feeling like an outsider.

In my family, the right relationship choices were clear. My younger sister, Carol, was engaged to an accountant. My older sister, Mary, married her high school sweetheart, a firefighter and Army veteran. Respectable. Predictable. Familiar. Joe was a good man, but he didn't check these boxes. So, I made a different choice.

I don't regret the choice, but I carried the quiet sadness of letting Joe go. His love helped me believe in myself, and even after I moved on, it stayed with me—a small reminder of being seen, tucked away in my heart.

Chapter 3

Belonging

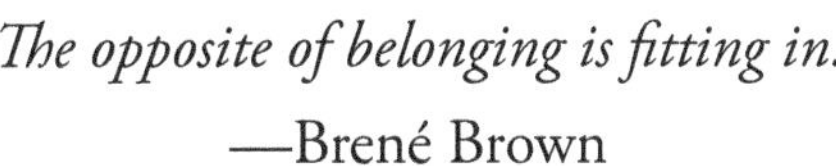

The opposite of belonging is fitting in.
—Brené Brown

It was late. The only light came from the streetlight filtering through the blinds. I sat wrapped in a blanket on the couch, eating Ben & Jerry's straight from the pint, waiting for John to return home. I'd lost count of how many nights I sat in that same spot in the three years since we were married, wondering if he'd been in an accident. Wondering if he'd come home at all.

The clock would tick past midnight, then 1, sometimes 2 a.m. Eventually, John would walk through the door, usually with alcohol on his breath and an excuse on his lips. A hockey game he couldn't miss. A last-minute shift at the bar where he worked part-time. A friend who needed him. Always a reason not to come home.

But this night was different. This time, I knew I would never be waiting on that couch again. Our marriage was over. It had been for a while. Truthfully, I am not sure if it ever really began.

John walked in as I tossed the last of the melted Phish Food in the trash. I looked at him, more sad than angry. I was too tired for anything else. I told him I was moving out the next day. He didn't argue. He didn't seem surprised. Relieved, maybe. I was twenty-nine.

I met John in college.

It was the fall semester at UMass. Joe and I had recently broken up. I was halfway through my bachelor's degree, struggling through my first Economics class—a subject I knew absolutely nothing about. John sat a couple of seats ahead of me and one row over. Handsome, well-dressed, with an easy smile. He seemed entirely at ease, both in himself and in the classroom. He joked with the professor and brought a kind of lightness to the room—a stark contrast to my serious, studious self.

It was several weeks before we even spoke. I didn't have much time to socialize between my job at CVS, a long commute, and the demands of school. My days were full. But that day, a Friday, a few fellow students convinced me to join them at the campus pub. My birthday was approaching, so I agreed to go. We gathered around a sticky table in the corner of the dark, well-worn pub and ordered a pitcher of beer. Never mind that I wasn't legal drinking age. I had been using a fake ID since I was sixteen.

John arrived a short while later with a group of friends. In high school, these guys were definitely the jocks, each of them wearing a football or hockey jacket embroidered with their names, numbers, and high school mascots. I glanced over and thought, *not my type*, though I'm not sure I actually had a type.

It wasn't long before our two groups began talking, and John directed his bright smile, handsome face, and outgoing personality toward me. He was talkative and charming. He shared that he lived in Revere, a city not unlike Somerville with a lower-middle-class, blue-collar population—densely populated and not entirely safe.

Much to my surprise, John asked for my phone number a couple of beers later. I was flustered and flattered as I wrote it down in my notebook and tore the page out unevenly. I left the pub at dusk. I was sure I would never hear from him again.

As I walked to catch the train, watching the last of the sun set, I pondered this young man I had just met. John was magnetic, shiny in a way that drew people in. I couldn't help but contrast him with Joe. Joe was mature, imposing at 6 ft. 8 in., with a sardonic wit. He was more of an acquired taste. Joe's presence was grounding. John's was unnerving. It seemed like everyone, including our economics professor, wanted John to shine his light on them.

Even then, I sensed something familiar in his ease—the kind of belonging I had always chased but never quite found.

So, when he called later that evening, I was rattled. I already sensed how easy it would be to get swept away by his charm.

We had one phone in our house—a bright yellow relic from the 1970s in the dining room, with a long cord you could drag down the hall for the little privacy that existed in the days before call waiting and long before mobile phones. When it rang after dinner, my sister Carol grabbed it. Fridays rarely passed in our house without an argument over the phone. "Susan, it's John something?" she called from the dining room. Handing me the receiver, she mouthed, "Who is John something?" I shrugged, took the phone, and walked as far as the yellow cord would reach.

The handsome hockey player from Economics had called after all. We started dating shortly after that phone call.

Almost immediately, John seemed an obvious choice for a future husband—the nice Italian boy I met in college, the kind of boy my family approved of. He was the model of the boy next door. The type of person it made sense to marry. After dating for just a few months, I saw how being with John would finally help me belong in the world I grew up in—how marrying him might unlock the approval I had spent a lifetime chasing.

But early on, I knew it was an illusion. John never saw me the way Joe had. Joe understood the real me—my intelligence, my ambition, and my imperfections. John loved the idea of me, the version that complemented his world—the package. He wasn't interested in the details of who I actually was. He thrived on attention, loved being loved, and rarely looked inward. His charm was magnetic but shallow, the kind that could fill a room without ever truly connecting.

Still, the promise of belonging felt worth the risk of disappearing into the white space of my own life. The irony is deeply sad. Even after years of feeling unseen by my family, I still cared what they thought. I was still trying, still hoping that if I made the right choice in a partner, I would finally matter.

From the start, dating John made more sense to others than it did to me. On paper, we were so much more alike than Joe and I had been. We came from similar backgrounds, shared the same cultural shorthand, and looked like the kind of couple that belonged together. His ease and comfort made me more approachable, where my ambition, intelligence, and self-reliance had always set me apart.

The very things Joe had seen and loved in me, the qualities that made me uniquely me, were dimmed by John's light. But his likability made me easier to explain, easier to place. It was as if I became more likable, more relatable because of him. With John, my story finally fit the family narrative—predictable, respectable, safe. In his reflection, I became visible, not necessarily to him, but to others.

I had felt seen, understood, and loved by Joe. With John, it was never about him seeing me. It was about others accepting me now that I was in a relationship that made sense to them. That acceptance came at a cost. I traded authenticity for approval.

John and I fell into a compatible routine. We finished college and got engaged. John's popularity had become my popularity. Our lives were full—traveling, gathering with friends, attending events, immersing ourselves in the easy rhythm of our twenties. Somewhere along the way, the lightness that first drew me in became the center of gravity I couldn't step out of. It was effortless to orbit around John, whose joy and ease made everything feel breezy. He rarely took anything seriously, including his career, which didn't bother me at the time. I had enough drive for both of us.

Around John, my personal identity was tenuous. It lacked the self-assuredness of my professional identity. It existed primarily within the warmth of his circle—his charm, his confidence, his ability to draw people in. I revolved around him, sustained by the story I had constructed: that this was a life of my choosing.

The truth was harder to face. I was living inside his narrative, not my own. My sense of self had become defined through him. It's easy to lose your own story inside someone else's when that story feels safer than your own. It was captivating, not in a healthy way, but in a clinging, hold-on-for-dear-life way. Letting go felt dangerous. If I did, I feared I'd plunge back into obscurity—back to not belonging, to not feeling part of something larger than myself.

That fear wasn't new. It reached back to childhood, to the quiet ache of being unseen. The story of John and me was less about love and more about escaping the fear of emotional invisibility. Being with John gave me a sense of connectedness, of finally fitting in. Childhood emotional neglect is powerful. No matter how strong my ego or how solid my professional identity had become, inside I was still that nine-year-old girl—just wanting her parents to notice that she was deaf in one ear.

John and I got married in 1988, following the script that was unconsciously written from the moment we met. I knew this wasn't the right ending to this story, but it was too late. As I stood at the back of the church on our wedding day, I whispered to my father, "Dad, I'm not sure this is a good decision." He didn't miss a beat. "Too late, Susan, let's go," he said, looking at me seriously. And we walked down the aisle, smiling, pretending.

The loneliness that settled over me on our wedding day, as we took the dance floor for the first time as husband and wife, never did lift.

It would take time to understand that being alone was far less painful than feeling lonely beside someone who couldn't truly see me.

Achievement had always been my refuge. Long before John, I had learned to find worth in hard work—at school, at CVS—anywhere effort might be rewarded with a sense of belonging or being seen. Work kept me grounded, no matter what was swirling around me.

I started working in Human Resources around the time I met John. HR came naturally to me; I was good at it, and I enjoyed it. It showed. My career had started its upward trajectory a couple of years before our wedding, when I was hired as the Human Resources manager at Ziff-Davis Publishing Company—a glossy empire of magazines and power. You could still smoke in your office then, and not drinking at lunch was considered impolite.

My cubicle was perched high in one of Boston's tallest skyscrapers, in an elegant office that matched the ambitious, high-achieving culture of Ziff-Davis. Stepping off the elevator on the thirtieth floor and into that beautifully appointed space took my breath away. It was nearly a 360-degree view from where I stood. You could see Cambridge, Back Bay, and even the airport. It was stunning, almost unreal. I couldn't believe I had been hired. It was beyond my wildest dreams, far from those school cafeteria days, sitting in the near dark, eating cheese and pickle sandwiches with Mary.

My boss, Carolyn, was sharp-edged, her glasses perpetually perched at the end of her nose, a cigarette always smoldering in the ashtray. She did not suffer fools, which she made clear from our first meeting. She also made it clear that I was barely qualified for the role, but she liked me, my brains, and my ambition, so she gave me the chance. In no uncertain terms, she let me know, not so subtly, that I best not disappoint her.

Carolyn was smart, tough, and unapologetically in charge. It was from her and this job that my professional identity solidified. I learned how to succeed in this highly competitive environment, how to interact at the most senior levels, and how to build credibility not just with policies but with intelligence and insight. I was not a stranger to hard work, but Ziff-Davis took it to a new level—and I excelled.

Working at Ziff-Davis was equally challenging and exhilarating. The company was innovating and expanding at a breakneck pace, with endless opportunities. My role grew just as rapidly. I soon managed a team and supported multiple business units, each with small HR teams reporting to me. As with my early job at CVS and my academic success, achievement in HR fueled my desire for more. At work, I felt entirely like myself—my professional identity forged through competence, agency, and the thrill of rising to meet the next challenge. It was gratifying.

While I was isolated at home—spending far too many nights on the couch in the dark, my only companion a pint of Ben & Jerry's that doubled as dinner—my career continued to soar. In 1989, Carolyn stepped down as head of Human Resources for Ziff-Davis's Boston division, and I was promoted to take her place.

The company had grown rapidly since I joined—nearly seven hundred employees across three locations and a dozen-person HR team under my leadership. I hadn't disappointed Carolyn—far from it. My success overjoyed her, and she remained one of my biggest champions for years.

I had no illusions that this role would be easy. But at twenty-seven, I felt invincible, had yet to meet a professional or academic challenge I couldn't overcome, and needed a distraction from my disintegrating marriage. And I delivered. I stepped up, led the team, became an integral part of senior leadership, and earned recognition as a competent, composed HR executive. My job and my identity fused tightly into one. The more I succeeded; the more contagious success became.

As the roots of my professional identity deepened, I stood taller, became more assertive, and grew more confident. Like a tree storing energy all winter only to burst forth in spring, I began to shine independently. My brightness no longer depended solely on John's light.

But just as I had co-opted his popularity as mine, my success at work became his. He hijacked it for his own identity, a surrogate for his lackluster career. He loved the idea of me—the competent professional, the capable wife—as much as he loved the idea of us. My achievements shored up the version of himself he wanted the world to see.

John didn't exactly lack ambition. He lacked commitment. He liked to keep his options open, his schedule loose enough to meet the guys at a moment's notice or to pick up an extra shift at the bar, where he relished being the center of attention.

As my days grew longer and the demands of leadership intensified, the things that once drew me to John began to exhaust me. We were nearing thirty. My professional growth was far outpacing my personal growth. It was a conundrum. By day, I was composed, in charge, and energized. At home, I felt helpless, alone, unsure how to navigate. John remained rooted in the free-spirited rhythm of our early twenties. It was no longer endearing.

And yet, I was still dependent on him for a sense of inclusion. He was, after all, the star of the narrative I had written years earlier, the one in which I co-starred, and where being his wife meant that I mattered and was enough. Unwinding that story felt unfathomable, even if it had lost its plot. Until, one day, weeks before the fateful Phish Food evening, John's love of attention and playfulness tipped into something I couldn't recover from.

It was a family celebration on a warm summer evening, held in the beautifully landscaped yard of my aunt and uncle's lovely home. Cocktails by the pool, dinner in the gazebo, champagne flutes clinking above plates of shrimp cocktail. My aunts, uncles, and cousins were all dressed up. So was I—hair and makeup done, a carefully chosen outfit I still remember. I don't recall what we were celebrating. But I remember exactly how it ended.

I hadn't even finished my first glass of champagne when John's mischievousness turned toward me. Without warning, he picked me up and threw me into the pool, to the absolute horror of everyone watching. At that moment, I wanted to sink to the bottom and disappear. Not from embarrassment, though there was plenty of that. But from the crushing realization that John being John had reached its emotional limit. What once would have been playful now felt desperate—as though he was trying to hold on to something neither of us could name.

I could no longer sustain the narrative I had built around our marriage. Theorists call this *narrative identity*—the internal stories we construct to make sense of who we are.[14] The story I had clung to—that safety and security came from being with John—shattered that day. It unraveled quickly from there.

We separated and divorced within a year. Many were surprised, but not John. Not really. Looking back, I think he saw it coming before anyone else did. That pool moment—as humiliating as it

---

[14] Dan P. McAdams, *Power, Intimacy, and the Life Story: Personological Inquiries into Identity* (Guilford Press, 1988).

was—now feels like his last attempt to hold on. In a gesture that seemed to mirror what was happening between us, he held me over the water and let go. And when he did, I knew I was gone. I think he had hoped differently. But it was time for me to stop pretending.

So now, in addition to being the first in my family to go to college, I became the first to get divorced. Not exactly a milestone anyone celebrated. To my family, the pool incident was a prank gone wrong, not the culmination of years of disconnection. They still saw John as the "good choice," the one who made sense. Steady. Safe. Familiar. They didn't see the story I'd been living inside, or how completely it had collapsed.

But it wasn't just the marriage that ended. It was the death of a dream I had clung to for years, the belief that our marriage would be the foundation for a future I longed for. I grieved that dream. Even though some part of me always knew it was only ever a dream, letting it go still hurt. And when the dream disappeared, so did the version of myself that existed only in relationship to John.

No longer intertwined, our shared friends and familiar routines returned to their rightful owner. They had always been his.

I needed to redefine myself—this time, not in his shadow but in his absence. I focused on what I knew—self-reliance, a role I had played since childhood. I was the one who didn't need anyone, who could succeed without being seen. My marriage was over. The story had collapsed. What remained was the one part of my identity I could still count on—the self I had built at work.

At work, my identity was anchored in competence and control. It did not drift with the turmoil of my divorce.

It remained steady. The culture at Ziff-Davis was unrelenting, and without the distraction of a personal life, I was free to give even more of myself to it. My efforts were well-timed; we were preparing for a massive consolidation, bringing all our sites into one location over the next few years. It came with a mountain of new responsibilities layered on top of my already demanding role.

I moved into a small apartment a few miles from the office. It was in a refinished attic in an old Victorian house in a cute suburban neighborhood. I started an early-morning exercise routine to undo the damage from all those late-night pints of Ben & Jerry's that had punctuated much of my marriage.

I settled into a steady new rhythm. I was up by 5 a.m., at the gym by 6 a.m., in the office by 7:30 a.m., often staying well past dark. It was lonely. It was safe. It was the first time I had ever lived by myself. I remember closing the door that first night and realizing no one else had a key. It felt different, yet slightly familiar, stirring something in me that had lain quiet much of the time I was with John. I was free from anyone else's expectations.

I had been emotionally self-sufficient since childhood, retreating inward to protect myself from the hurt of being unseen. Being alone again reawakened what had always been missing: attention, attunement, and belonging. I was back where I began, and now, I was once again protecting myself from being misunderstood.

My family disapproved of the divorce. They lamented John's absence, criticized my choices, and blamed me. To them, he hadn't done anything unforgivable—just been himself, the charming, self-centered man they'd always known. Leaving him made me the one at fault. It seemed that wanting to be loved for being me was more than they believed I deserved—then, and perhaps ever.

They thought my ambitions were too lofty. I had a good job; wasn't that enough? Why the need for more? I avoided them. Our mutual friends—no longer mutual—avoided me.

Thank goodness for the sustaining power of my connection to Mary. I talked to her most days, sharing all of life's trials and tribulations. She grounded me and reminded me of what it means to feel seen for who you are. I was also sustained by a different kind of love, simpler and smaller in size, but just as powerful. My sisters had started their families. I was an auntie.

The arrivals of these babies filled me with happiness. When my first niece, Meghan, my older sister's daughter, was born, my younger sister and I ran down the hospital hallway, elbowing each other out of the way like teenagers, arguing loudly about who would hold her first. A few years later, I had three nephews, each one bringing their own joy and light.

Being an aunt became so much more than I ever expected. Maybe it was the timing—I was recently divorced, and being a mother myself felt distant, unlikely. Perhaps it was because I had grown up surrounded by the love of so many aunts and uncles and now understood what that meant.

Or maybe it was simply that being Auntie Susan was enough. It was acceptance without judgment, without condition—just love, joy, and connection. It steadied me as I kept moving forward, while my career remained my focus.

I stayed with Ziff-Davis for a few more years, eventually leaving for a bigger, more lucrative position that brought me closer to my dream of becoming a chief people officer by forty. I wore my professional identity like a mask. It was polished, secure, and fitted so well that I almost forgot it wasn't me.

Near the end of my time with Ziff-Davis, I met Ken. I wasn't looking to date, and marriage was nowhere on my radar. And Ken? He came with baggage—twice divorced, a recovering alcoholic, and a smoker. I'd sworn off smokers. And yet.

There was something about him. His deep work ethic, sharp intelligence, and hard-won life experience drew me in, not to mention his subtle charisma, not shiny like John, not unapproachable like Joe. He was real, easy to talk to; what you see is what you get with Ken. Plus, at 6 ft. 3 in., handsome with gorgeous blue eyes, he was hard to resist. We started hanging out casually—coffee after long days and low-key, easy dinners. I didn't expect to fall for him, but I did.

After dating a year or so, we moved in together. It was comfortable and natural. I didn't have to fit into Ken's world—I became his world. He didn't ask me to be anyone else. His love was steady and unconditional, and his sense of self was unwavering. Professionally, he was my equal, leading a large IT team with the same drive and intensity I brought to my own work.

My family rejected him early on. Still mourning John, they couldn't understand this choice, couldn't understand me. Ken didn't fit their expectations. But this time, I didn't care. I no longer needed to be accepted into their version of my life. This time, I chose for myself.

While I still had many doubts about getting married again, Ken surprised me one day as we walked through a beautiful park in the city, getting down on one knee to propose. I said yes. Six months later, we had a small, elegant ceremony.

I had long since abandoned the idea of being a mother. Even after meeting Ken, I couldn't quite picture it. Despite my deep love for my niece and nephews, I had never even changed a diaper. And then there was my career—my aspirations didn't neatly align with motherhood.

But with Ken, anything felt possible. We decided to have a baby.

I soon became pregnant with our daughter, Allison. The pregnancy was complicated from the outset. During my first trimester, morning sickness lasted all day, every day. A trash bucket was never far from my reach. When I finally made it through a day without getting sick, I was relieved—until a few weeks later when I woke up in the middle of the night with stabbing cramps. Fearing the worst, we went straight to the emergency room.

My doctor was on call that night. After a quick exam, she told me I was in preterm labor. I would have to take it easy or risk early delivery. I nodded automatically, but I didn't fully grasp what she meant until she put it directly: I was on bed rest for the rest of my pregnancy.

A year earlier, I had run a marathon. Now I was confined to the couch or the bed for four and a half months.

For someone who had always been in motion—ambitious, driven, managing people and deadlines—it was baffling to be sidelined in my own life. At first, I wanted to argue, to negotiate, to prove I could keep going. But there was no bargaining with my body, and the stakes were too high. I surrendered—I had no choice. I would not risk Allison's safety.

Day after day, the world carried on without me while I stayed still. Or at least my body did. My mind refused to stop. A fax machine sat on the table next to me, my laptop perched nearby, my phone always within reach. From the couch, I continued working, unwilling—or maybe unable—to fully let go of the identity that had carried me this far.

It was a preview of motherhood itself. The relentless call to surrender, to yield control, to trust that everything would be okay. I didn't know it then, but it was also a preview of another reckoning that lay ahead when my body would once again demand something that I couldn't outwork.

Allison arrived two weeks early. Her arrival brought us such happiness. She was healthy, beautiful, and worth every motionless day. She completed our little family. My personal life finally felt like it was mine.

My career still had a tight grip on me. Alli's arrival hadn't changed that. Ken and I were doing well professionally. We bought our first house, and a little over a year after Allison was born, I entered the C-suite—two years ahead of my goal.

We had it all. Careers, family, and a lovely home. My professional identity was central to who I was. It remained the most comfortable and familiar part of me. But I had begun curating a personal life that matched it. Our home was gorgeous, and every detail was carefully chosen to reflect our happiness, our success.

Motherhood was complicated for me. It had never been explicitly part of my plan. I adored our daughter, but incorporating *momma* into my identity didn't come naturally. I wasn't the mom with the playdate calendar or homemade snacks. I was still me, ambitious, driven, and in control, now with a diaper bag slung over one shoulder and my briefcase on the other. Deep down, I was afraid I would get the role of mom wrong—that I would raise Alli as I had been raised without a sense of belonging or visibility. Loved. But not seen.

Luckily, Allison was born a daddy's girl. Ken loved every minute of her adoration. She went to a day care we trusted, and we had a nanny who helped out in the early evenings. Our work schedules were demanding, but Alli always came first. She was safe. She was adored. She knew that she mattered.

At work, I was deeply fulfilled as a chief people officer. My ambition had not dimmed in the shadow of motherhood. I had struggled with imposter syndrome earlier in my career, but not this time. I quietly and confidently knew that I was meant for this role.

The financial technology company I worked for was a joint venture within a larger Fortune 500 firm. Joint ventures are notoriously tricky from a people and organizational perspective. I had developed deep expertise in organizational development since becoming an HR person many years earlier. I was well-suited to create and implement a people strategy to support the goals of this business. It was a dream job. Complex. Dynamic. Challenging.

Most of my colleagues on the executive team were men. All but one were older than me. Carolyn's mentorship had prepared me well to integrate into this team. I knew how to stand up for myself and could hold my own. There was much to do to merge these two diverse companies to form a unified brand and culture. I rolled up my sleeves and dug in. I built productive relationships, even some friendships, across the executive team and hired talented staff to support the business in achieving its ambitious strategy.

Ken and I negotiated Alli's day care drop-off. On days when I didn't drop off, I maintained my rigorous morning schedule, rising by 5 a.m., getting to the gym by 6 a.m., and arriving at my desk by 7:30 a.m. Most evenings, the nanny brought Alli home after day care to feed her dinner and get her ready for bed. One of us would always be home to relieve the nanny, usually Ken, to read Alli stories and put her to bed. I often arrived home to a quiet, dark house and a plate on the stove for me to reheat for dinner.

We fell into a rhythm, and the life we were building felt solid. I felt solid, no longer a prisoner in a story about my life, no longer only recognizable in relation to someone else. I was happy, fulfilled, and content.

But nothing stays the same for long. A year later, in the fall of 2001, everything changed.

The world was thrown into chaos on that unforgettable morning of September 11. I remember every detail. When we heard the news, my colleagues and I were in our weekly executive team meeting in Boston. Half of our team was based in lower Manhattan, all within view of the World Trade Center. Panic ensued. The hours and days that followed were surreal.

It was a time that tested every bit of my leadership as we navigated completely unfamiliar terrain—frantically working to steady our teams, support our people, and manage the business uncertainty that followed. The days got longer and the stress more acute, and my ability to distinguish one day from the next began to blur. My job further consumed me. It was the most challenging chapter of my career and one of my proudest.

It took nearly a year for the business to emerge from the turmoil and return to a steady state. Ken filled in the gaps at home during my absence, and Alli was too young to understand what had happened. Eventually, work and home settled into a new normal, though the events of 9/11 remain forever in our hearts and minds.

I turned forty that fall. The world had changed, and so had I.

After 9/11, my sense of importance at work intensified. My presence felt essential. I began to see myself as indispensable, crucial to the business's success. My professional identity had always been outsized. It was now overwhelming, leaving little room for anything else.

From the outside, everything appeared normal. Alli was thriving. Ken was steady, and his career continued to rise. But inside, something wasn't right—a sense of unease, an increasing discomfort. Subtle, at first, but a nagging, persistent knowing that I wasn't okay.

I ignored it. I tried to outwork it.

I pushed harder, not wiser. I stayed late, fabricating deadlines, whispering that whatever this was, it would pass. I just had to keep going. I found more reasons to stay later: another meeting, another email, another late night at the bar with colleagues who needed me. I told myself this was the price of success. This was what was required of the C-suite; it was normal, even when I knew it wasn't.

Alcohol numbed the choking sensation that something was wrong. That I was wrong. But it only worked temporarily and not without a cost—first my judgment and then my health.

By forty-two, the cracks were undeniable. I blamed burnout. The signs were similar. I was chronically exhausted, devoid of pleasure, and thoroughly hopeless. I couldn't see a way out. Working more didn't help, nor did self-medicating. I was trapped in the same loop—rinse and repeat, day after day.

Ken's patience wore thin with the drinking, the long hours, and my growing irrationality. A quiet air of discontent hung over us. He all but stopped talking to me, his frustration palpable. Without the grounding of Ken's steadiness, I frayed further. My clarity dulled, and my confidence at work, once so deeply rooted, began to waver, replaced by uncertainty. I didn't turn to my family. I no longer sought their approval, and I knew better than to expect their understanding. The distance I had once mourned had become necessary and protective, especially now.

The core of my identity—anchored in competence, control, and composure—was deteriorating, and so was my sense of self. The mask I had worn for decades no longer fit, yet I didn't know how to take it off. I didn't know who I was without it.

Six months later, my collapse was complete. I was alone, sobbing in a hotel bathroom, staring into a mirror at a woman I barely recognized.

Despite the signs, I never saw it coming.

The relentless, silent undoing of perimenopause.

I had relied on my carefully constructed identity for safety. Yet it was that mask that kept me from recognizing my unraveling.

Psychologist Susan Harter wrote that when our self-worth is tied to competence, failure doesn't just feel like failure—it feels like collapse.[15] She was right.

---

[15] Harter, *Construction of the Self.*

Chapter 4

The Long Exhale

Pause. Breathe. Repair your universe.
—Pema Chödrön

The image of the colorful hand-painted table leg sailing through the air as the house was demolished imprinted on my mind as I drove Alli to school. I thought wistfully about the little gallery where we bought the table, just off of Newbury Street in Boston. It took years to buy the matching chairs, buying one at a time whenever we had some extra money.

As we idled at a red light, I was consumed by my thoughts. We would buy another dining room table. But it wouldn't be the same—nothing would be. Gone with that table were the stories about how we so thoughtfully collected each piece, the memories of the mismatched chairs, the search for the perfect color, or the time we spent debating which piece we should get next.

Allison was chattering away in the back seat. She could hardly wait to get to school that morning so she could tell her friends how she had helped drive the big truck. Her enthusiasm for demolishing the house snapped me out of my daydream. I laughed, her energy contagious. Many days in those months after the fire, Alli's delight was the portal to our previous life, like the wardrobe in the movie *The Chronicles of Narnia*. She reminded us that we could find our way back to happiness.

I had barely come to a stop when she practically jumped from the car in front of her school, her excitement propelling her toward the crowd of kids. She turned to wave, smiling brightly. I waved and drove back to the bland, cookie-cutter surroundings of the temporary apartment we had been living in for many months.

I made some tea and sat down in front of the borrowed laptop where I had spent weeks documenting every last possession—spreadsheet after spreadsheet, each one a record of a loss. I double checked to make sure a dining room table was on there. It was. I pictured our future table, plain and functional, like my surroundings. Sigh.

I couldn't bear to review another spreadsheet that morning. I opened my email. I had not responded to the inquiry from the consulting firm. I read it again.

Are you still interested?

Was I still interested? Yes. I definitely was. Was I ready? I didn't think so.

Menopause's assault on my body had eased for a time leading up to the fire. After months of sleepless nights and unpredictable moods, I had begun to feel steadier, as is often the case in the transition to postmenopause when hormone levels become less erratic. But my progress was erased by the devastation of the fire. The shock and stress reignited my symptoms, leveling me again. Trauma and menopause move through the body in eerily similar ways, dysregulating neurological functioning and wreaking havoc physically, psychologically, and socially.

I had received a menopause diagnosis but no treatment. Hormone therapy was never discussed. I was young and my doctor seemed comfortable that I could manage on my own. Most days, it seemed like little of the former me remained—no career, no closet full of beautiful clothes, no remaining external markers to signal that I still mattered somewhere. The relentless effort to stay upright had rendered me frail, alone, exposed. I no longer even had the comfort of those beautiful clothes to hide from my pain.

How could I possibly say yes to this opportunity? How could I not?

I sipped my almost cold tea, my chest tight with anxiety. Could I trust that the worst had passed this time? I had been here before. Normalcy felt tenuous. I was trying to put one foot in front of the other but was scared that the ground wouldn't hold me. I was surviving but not yet healing.

Doctors hadn't been particularly helpful. I'd been told to manage my menopausal symptoms on my own, but managing meant enduring, as it so often does for women. My symptoms were minimized—dismissed as no big deal—despite how debilitating they were, compounded by my body's response to trauma. I was depleted, too exhausted to advocate for myself. It felt as though I was standing still while life moved on around me, waiting in a dim hallway for a door that never opened.

The good news, the small light at the end of the hallway: the process of reconciling the material loss and damage from the fire was nearly complete. Our insurance claims were almost done.

With the remains of the original house now demolished, the new house build would begin immediately.

I knew it was also time for me to rebuild. I had to free myself from liminality, whether I was ready or not. It was time to find my way out of the metaphorical hallway where I had been imprisoned for months.

I took another sip of tea and held my breath as I responded to the email.

Yes, I am still interested. When can I start?

I slowly exhaled and wondered if this might be the first step in healing.

Returning to work was familiar. Would working again help pull me out of this abyss of despair? Maybe resurrecting a piece of my professional identity would help me find myself again. I knew that the part-time contract work was a far cry from the C-suite, but after more than a year and a half of being unemployed and adrift, this opportunity gave me a glimmer of hope. If not the step toward healing that I needed, it was a life raft; it would hopefully at least keep me from slipping further under.

As my first day approached, I struggled to shake the emotional numbness that had taken me prisoner. I wanted to feel excited, energized, like the old me. I was moving forward, however small a step it was. I had been teetering on the edge of dissociation before the fire. My cognitive function was distorted, not operating on all cylinders. The fire compounded the neurological chaos that had started with menopause.

My brain had been hijacked in two different directions at once. It is not widely understood that menopause is a neurological event, not just a hormonal one. With declining estrogen, the brain loses access to one of its most essential fuels.[16] Memory, mood, and focus all suffer. Trauma also reshapes the brain. It floods the amygdala, dulls the prefrontal cortex, and disrupts the hippocampus.[17]

I hadn't lost my mind. My brain was being rewired. I was caught in a perfect storm of biological, neurological, and emotional disruption. It was going to take more than a new job to free me from the throes of this tempest.

Pema Chödrön is often quoted as saying, "When things fall apart, that's when the real work begins."[18]

I had picked up her book on a day when I was wandering aimlessly through the local bookstore, its title, *When Things Fall Apart*, calling to me. I hoped to find an answer in its pages, a solution that would free me. Instead, I found myself wondering, day after day, *What is my real work—the inner work I need to do to reclaim myself?* My career had always been my refuge. It had saved me after my divorce in my twenties. And even earlier as a young adult, my job at CVS fueled my belief in myself that I could do something more, be something more.

Maybe, despite the wildly different context, I would find myself again in this new job. As a symbolic gesture, I returned to Bloomingdale's and repurchased the same outfit I had chosen months earlier for the first day that never came. It was a classic silk Eileen Fisher outfit, part of an annual collection. Timeless,

---

[16] Lisa Mosconi, *The Menopause Brain* (Penguin Random House, 2024).

[17] Bessel van der Kolk, *The Body Keeps the Score: Brain, Mind, and Body in the Healing of Trauma* (Viking, 2014).

[18] Pema Chodron, *When Things Fall Apart: Heart Advice for Difficult Times* (Shambhala Publications, 2000).

reliable, dependable. As if wearing the same clothes could erase all that had collapsed in between. As if I could dress myself back into who I once was.

I wasn't naïve enough to believe that a new outfit was going to rescue me, but it did help ground me in something normal, familiar—at least for the moment. I didn't know where to start the kind of work Pema suggested, but I knew it wasn't at Bloomingdale's. And then a friend who had recently endured her own trauma suggested acupuncture.

Acupuncture? I was skeptical. The idea that a handful of needles could reach the part of me consumed by the chaos of the last eighteen months and heal it felt preposterous. However, I was out of options with nothing to lose. Maybe these tiny needles could begin to stitch together what still felt so frayed inside me. I made an appointment with Huang Yu; a Chinese acupuncturist trained in traditional Eastern medicine.

Her waiting room was calm and welcoming. The soft sound of a water fountain soothed me the moment I sat down. When I entered her treatment room, her gentle presence brought tears to my eyes. Huang Yu greeted me with quiet compassion and a calm confidence, a sense of knowing that she could help me.

Remarkably, she didn't ask me to explain my current state. She didn't require justification or proof. Huang Yu met me exactly where I was and began her work, one needle at a time. She was methodical and deliberate, targeting the organs where my stress lived like a clenched fist. I barely felt the movement of the needles, but when I stood up afterward, something in me had shifted. It wasn't dramatic. I felt a release as if my body had exhaled after holding its breath for far too long. I burst into tears.

In just one session, the numbness began to lift ever so slightly. I returned week after week. As the needles opened the channels in my body, I began to release old stories and reimagine a new narrative. In this new story, the polished image I had so carefully maintained was gone. Even the outfit I had so meticulously chosen—twice—wasn't going to bring it back.

I began to understand that resilience was no longer my goal. My old self was not what I was seeking. As my body freed itself of seemingly endless stress and tension, my mind became clearer. I now knew that returning to who I used to be was no longer possible, but who would I be instead? How would a new story emerge? What would help me to rewrite a new narrative? Most days it still seemed impossible.

And then one day, lying on Huang Yu's table, as the needles worked their magic, I could sense it. My determination. It was still there. Like a faint pulse, underneath the stillness. My will was the indestructible thread that had persisted through the fire, through menopause, through loss. I could feel it again. It felt different. It wasn't pushing me toward competence or achievement; it was pushing me toward compassion. Toward grace. Not the will to do; the will to be.

Acupuncture rebalanced my energy and helped regulate my nervous system. It freed me to step out of the paralysis of fear and move through the threshold space between identities, out of the prolonged liminality, where the old self no longer fits and the new one has yet to emerge.

It was as if I had been sitting backward on a train, watching where I had been, unable to see where I was going. Only now could I turn around and glimpse what lay ahead. My suffering,

I came to learn, wasn't a detour. It was the path—an evolving, moment-by-moment unfolding of all that I had known into something new and unknown, not in spite of the trauma but shaped by it.

As Prentis Hemphill has written, "We don't heal to become who we were. We heal to become who we are."[19] For this, I didn't need a plan or a roadmap back. I needed a practice. Acupuncture gave me a steady ground on which I could begin to rebuild—clarity, calmness, and a deep receptivity. It activated my dormant sense of agency. I no longer muddled through each day dazed by grief or imprisoned by trauma.

As Bessel van der Kolk explains in *The Body Keeps the Score*, trauma is stored in the body.[20] I could feel this truth in my own muscles and nerves—it had reshaped how I moved through the world. To continue what acupuncture had begun, I would need to embody my healing—because reclaiming my body was the only way to reclaim myself.

Yoga was the practice I chose, or perhaps it chose me. Acupuncture cracked open the door in the hallway I had long been stalled in; yoga would teach me how to walk through it—integrating breath, movement, and spirit into a path of becoming.

I returned to my mat, not to the yoga I previously knew in the C-suite or in the early days after my resignation. That yoga was a punishing ninety-minute heated vinyasa practice. It mirrored my

---

[19] Prentis Hemphill, *What It Takes to Heal: How Transforming Ourselves Can Change the World* (Random House, 2025).

[20] van der Kolk, *Body Keeps the Score.*

relentless need to outperform, to prove my worth both inside and outside the office.

Those studios were heated to near unbearable levels, packed wall-to-wall with people pushing themselves to the brink. Mats were arranged with military precision, the air thick with humidity, eucalyptus, and ambition. The moment you stepped on your mat, it felt like boot camp.

That wasn't yoga as a form of mindfulness or healing. It was an endurance workout with a sprinkling of yogic philosophy. The yoga was not the point. The sweat was. The sweatier, the better. Each practice was a test of will, a competition with myself. Sun salutation after sun salutation, it wasn't about feeling, it was about surviving.

I would leave soaked, spent, and feeling worthy. I loved it.

I had long ago internalized that worth had to be earned, again and again. This strenuous type of yoga fit nicely in that narrative. That drive to earn my worth didn't stop at the office. It followed me onto my mat, into my life.

But now, I needed something different, nourishing, healing. I found my way to Rolf Gates.

A former US Army Ranger and social worker turned yoga teacher, Rolf is deeply grounded, equal parts regular guy and spiritual guide. Ironically, I first encountered him a couple of years earlier in the power yoga world. When I eventually returned to my mat, his teaching had softened.

His yoga was slower, more introspective, and rooted in inquiry. It was less about striving and more about seeing. He weaves yogic philosophy into everything he teaches, not just the postures but also the principles that underpin them: Yamas and Niyamas, meditation, and self-study.

Rolf teaches from his own lived experience, especially his recovery from addiction, offering a yoga practice infused with humility, acceptance, and self-compassion. His focus is not on transformation through effort, as it once had been, but on transformation through letting go. He became my guru as I stepped into the next phase of healing, toward being rather than doing.

My first time back on my mat after the fire was at the Kripalu Center for Yoga and Health. Kripalu is a retreat center nestled deep into the Berkshire Mountains in Western Massachusetts. Housed in a former Jesuit monastery, Kripalu is a sparse, no-frills facility with the religious undertones of an ashram. Its softness is welcoming and open, while its deep roots give it a balance of strength and structure.

I was raised Catholic. My family never missed a Sunday at church, a sacrament, a holy day, or Sunday school. I believe the deep values of the Catholic tradition offer lifelong guidance—whether you practice faithfully or not. By this stage in life, I had drifted from the church. Yet, as I stood in the doorway of one of the preeminent spiritual centers of yoga in the United States, I felt the spiritual pull of my surroundings, as if the power of yoga in its completeness was beckoning me from beyond the doorway, not as a series of challenging postures practiced in punishing heat, but as a way of life.

Yoga, at its essence, means union. A holistic yoga practice moves beyond the asanas, the physical poses, to integrate spirituality and mindfulness. Acupuncture had unlocked my belief in the power of energetic and spiritual healing. As I lingered in the doorway upon arriving at Kripalu, looking out at the backdrop of the beautiful mountains, the foliage vibrant, bright with color,

I felt like I had been here before. It had a strangely familiar feeling, as if I belonged here, as if I had finally come home.

I grabbed my bag and my yoga mat and stepped over the threshold, unsure of what was beyond, though sure that it was where I was meant to be. I got settled in my room, a small dorm-like space with a single bed, so simple and unadorned that I wondered if monks still roamed the halls of Kripalu. Class was about to start, and I did not want to be late. I hurried to the studio.

The studio was warm and dimly lit, the smell of incense drifting through a scattering of mats. Its marked difference from the yoga studios I knew was a touch disorienting. I found a spot for my mat and was relieved when I saw Rolf take his place in the front of the room.

We began our practice with a seated meditation. We were there for so long that I wondered if I had mistakenly signed up for a meditation-only retreat. I was new to meditation and found it challenging to sit still. Quieting my mind felt nearly impossible. Once we started moving, the vinyasa was comforting, and I eased into the flow. Rolf's words washed over me as we moved through the opening series of asanas—the sun salutations.

"Root down to reach higher," he said, as we stood tall in extended mountain pose, arms high in the air.

"Shine your heart forward, reach a little higher, and shine brighter."

"We can live in the light with the same ease in which we live in the darkness."

"Who are we not to shine?"

His words landed not as an instruction but as an invitation. In this invitation, I understood that I was not at Kripalu just to heal from the trauma and grief of the fire or the loss of my identity and health to menopause. I was there to begin the process of shedding my false self, the performative mask that I had worn for so long and so convincingly. It had become indistinguishable from my true self. Peeling away the mask to discover what was underneath would not happen quickly, as a single act of bravery, but rather as a slow, sacred unfurling.

Where I once turned to the Bible and rosary beads, I now found meaning in the *Yoga Sutras*, a foundational text of yogic philosophy, and in my spiritual bead necklace, a mala. Yogic philosophy is vast and astounding. The Sutras are layered, poetic, and expansive in scope, offering insight into the nature of the mind, the process of liberation, and the path to spiritual awakening.

The first *Yoga Sutra* reads: "With humility—with an open heart and mind—we embrace the sacred study of yoga."[21] Embracing who I might become through yoga intrigued me and helped me release the false notion I held tight—that healing was about returning to sometime, someone, from the past. I quickly learned that my yoga practice was not about making me feel better. It was about making me feel.

Buddhist teacher Thich Nhat Hanh is often quoted: "No mud, no lotus."[22]

The lotus flower is a timeless symbol of spiritual unfolding. It rises from the mud, drawing energy from within, opening into its true self, petal by petal. Thriving not in spite of the darkness but because of it. That first day on my mat at Kripalu, I felt something

---

[21] Nischala Joy Devi, *The Secret Power of Yoga* (Harmony Books, 2022).

[22] Thich Nhat Hanh, *No Death, No Fear: Comforting Wisdom for Life* (Penguin, 2003).

stirring deep inside as I reached higher, my arms outstretched, standing taller, and shining brighter.

Who was I really? I didn't know. As my mask dissolved, would I uncover my essence rising from the mud, like the lotus flower?

Another thing became clear during my time at Kripalu: Returning to health wasn't a destination; it wasn't a point in time. It was deeply layered with consciousness, humility, and acceptance. Healing was stepping into the light and embracing authenticity and vulnerability, no longer hidden by the safety of competence and composure.

I had spent a lifetime inside of a role, my true self invisible even to me. I would learn in time that yoga would challenge me to exist without hiding. I had to learn to allow grace to happen, not hoping for it, not trying to force it, not believing I had to earn it, just stepping back and letting it in. It was time to shine.

This was a new beginning, from trauma to stillness, from stillness to self. Periodically, in a vinyasa practice, you pause at the top of your mat, standing in stillness for a moment before moving again—a breath between action and inaction.

In this moment, Rolf often says, "Let your sand settle and your water clear."

I was starting to understand the real work ahead of me. I had to release a lifetime of stories about who I believed I was and drop any remaining pretense of who I thought I should be. In Buddhist teachings, this is anattā—the principle of no fixed self. Things end. Nothing holds lasting substance.[23] There was no going back.

---

[23] Devi, *Secret Power of Yoga*.

I needed to learn to meet myself where I was and trust, as the *Yoga Sutras* teach, that I already had everything I needed. Yoga freed me to explore and embrace the freedom of letting go. Releasing my grip on all the things that had made me feel like me was scary but also strangely comforting. As I stepped beyond the dualities of hope and fear, I understood how my suffering had been the path all along.

I would come to understand that yoga had shown me the way to post-traumatic growth—a concept that I had never heard of at the time.[24] I was growing and changing, not because of the trauma but because of my struggle to make sense of it; not in spite of what I lost, but because of what was revealed in its absence.

As I moved from the numbness that had enveloped me for so many months back toward something that felt like a truer self, I would rest in savasana, the final pose of a yoga practice, astonished. Astonished by all that I had lost and even more so by the fact that what was gone no longer pulled at me. My old self, my old world, had vanished and I didn't miss it.

In this freedom, I began to understand that letting go of what I had long believed was my fixed self—the one who was always striving, aching to fit in, and trying to prove her worth—created possibilities that had never seemed available before the chaos of the last eighteen months.

How would I write this new life story? What would remain? What would I discard?

---

[24] Richard G. Tedeschi and Lawrence G. Calhoun, "Posttraumatic Growth: Conceptual Foundations and Empirical Evidence," *Psychological Inquiry* 15, no. 1 (2004): 1–18.

It was a time full of possibilities. My professional identity as I had once known it was gone. The personal narrative that had supported it lay in tatters. My relationships with others felt uncertain as a new version of me—a truer yet unfamiliar one—began to emerge.

The idea that such transformation could arise from suffering is as old as time. But it was only now dawning on me. I had been playing small, focused on resilience—focused on getting back to normal, returning to my premenopause, pre-fire baseline—without realizing that I was capable of so much more.

This opening, once revealed, ignited unexpected changes in many aspects of my life.

Psychologists Richard Tedeschi and Lawrence Calhoun have studied this phenomenon, and their framework outlines how post-traumatic growth tends to emerge.[25] Yoga helped me realize these shifts in my own life—not all at once and not always with certainty, but as subtle signs of growth and change. My sand had settled. My water had cleared.

My grief remained, but it now lived within a larger framework of wisdom—wisdom born from that very grief, which had once brought me to my knees but was now carrying me forward. I lost count of the number of times since the fire that I said silently or aloud, "If I can live through that, I can live through anything."

From a young age, a core tenet of my identity had been self-reliance—but not like this. This experience had developed muscles I hadn't known existed. It wasn't just about knowing

[25] Richard G. Tedeschi and Lawrence G. Calhoun, "The Posttraumatic Growth Inventory: Measuring the Positive Legacy of Trauma," *Journal of Traumatic Stress* 9 (1996): 455–71.

I could handle a difficult situation—I had always known that. It was discovering a different kind of strength, one that came not from control but from surrender. Not from knowing what to do but from accepting that not all situations need to be handled. Some just need to be lived.

Living without a road map—or at least a carefully mapped-out plan—had never been my modus operandi. My life hadn't always gone according to plan, but I always had one. And if I was sidelined by a detour, like my divorce from John, I could pretty quickly regroup and get back on track.

This time, I had no track to return to. For a long time, that made me deeply uncomfortable. But now, I had turned a corner. I began to savor the freedom of simply living—open to what might be possible.

I decided to embrace my consulting role, not as a stopgap but as a deliberate next step. I joined the firm full-time to lead the Talent Management practice. The pay and prestige were a fraction of what I was used to in the C-suite, but so was the pressure to perform. In its place, I had time, flexibility, and far less stress. For the first time in years, work didn't consume me. I was able to leave it at the office and be truly present at home.

My health had stabilized in a postmenopausal state, but I was far from fully well. Tending to my well-being became a priority. Time for yoga and acupuncture was non-negotiable.

My rebuilding was happening in parallel with the reconstruction of our home. But we began to see that the dream house of our past was no longer necessary to define our success or prove we had made it. We built a simpler house and resisted filling it with expensive, unnecessary things. I still missed the red

Prada bag I had lost in the fire, but I no longer needed what it once represented.

My growth in how I related to others was slower—more painstaking. Defining myself through the eyes of others—and my deep longing to be seen—felt like part of my DNA. Unwinding this took time. It wasn't linear. I meandered through this domain the longest, taking two steps forward and one back. Rarely the other way around. Like a tortoise, slow and steady.

This part of my development would emerge later when I returned to leadership—softer, less ambitious, and more compassionate, not just with others but with myself. It also quietly reshaped my interactions with my family. Over time, I began releasing my long-held desire to fit in, to prove myself, to matter. I let go of the need for approval, at least for a time.

Self-reliance, new possibilities, and relationships with others—my growth in each area came together in pieces over time, like a thousand-piece puzzle on the coffee table you spend just five minutes a day on. But each piece, each milestone, enhanced my appreciation for life itself, the last of the growth areas outlined by Tedeschi and Calhoun's framework.[26]

Gone were the superficial markers by which I had once measured success. In their place was a growing comfort with the ordinary. A morning without chaos, a quiet evening at home, a walk without urgency. Life was no longer measured by how much we earned, how important our titles were, or how perfect our house looked.

---

[26] Tedeschi and Calhoun, "The Posttraumatic Growth Inventory."

I was learning to let go of the illusion of perfection and embrace the messiness of life—whole, imperfect, and real.

Events that once felt like they might destroy me had instead altered my basic assumptions about life and its meaning. My existential crisis had become my existential growth. I now deeply understood what I had started to discern from my teachers in this season of my life. That when things come apart it is not the end—it is an opportunity.

Nearly two years after my resignation and a year after I stood on the lawn that chilly April night in my pajamas, watching our house burn to the ground, the new house was finished. It wasn't the same house. It was simpler, lighter, and less fussy. Just as I had learned that returning to who I was two years earlier was no longer possible, rebuilding the same house wasn't either. Having a perfect house no longer consumed me. It no longer held a grip on my identity. It didn't make me someone who mattered.

When we moved to the house initially, we needed two moving trucks. We had so many things—more clothes and purses than I care to admit, more toys than Alli could ever play with, and of course, the entire dining room of hand-painted furniture covered in those bright, beautiful flowers I adored.

This time, we packed Ken's Jeep with our clothes, essentials, and Allison's toys and said goodbye to the bleak corporate apartment we had called home for the last year.

It was a short ride. Allison couldn't wait to see her new room; she was bubbling over with delight. Ken and I were more contained, maybe even a bit anxious. A year earlier, the house had felt like a fresh start, full of hope and promise. Now, it was just a house, a place to make new memories, celebrate milestones, and continue healing. It wasn't a beginning or an end. It had no power to define who we were becoming.

We walked through the door without ceremony. No grand celebration. No dramatic moment of arrival. Just a deep exhale. We smiled as Allison took off for her room.

She had turned eight a few weeks earlier. Our first celebration in the newly constructed house was her belated birthday party —a '70s theme, complete with a game of Twister and cupcakes decorated with peace signs, hearts, and smiley faces. As the kids' laughter echoed off the unadorned walls and windows, I stared at the cupcakes. *Peace. Love. Joy.* Their message echoed in my heart, speaking to the child inside me and reminding me that I was no longer stuck in the past. I was arriving—perhaps for the first time—as who I was becoming.

Yoga has taught me to meet myself in the present. But yoga is not just what happens on the mat. It's a practice of choosing, again and again, how to move through the world. At that moment, standing in our new kitchen and gazing at the cupcakes, I felt more whole than I had in years.

But wholeness is not a finish line. It's like yoga, a daily opportunity. A practice. Each day forward is a choice—a chance to meet life with grace, gratitude, and joy. Healing was not about becoming whole once and for all. It was about returning to the mat, to the breath, to myself—again and again.

Chapter 5

Becoming Again

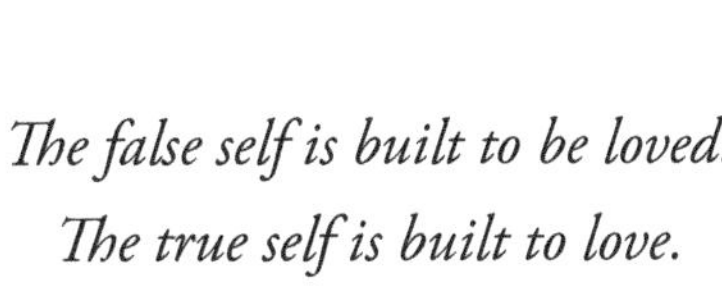

The false self is built to be loved.
The true self is built to love.
—Rolf Gates

Peace. Love. Joy. The messages from the birthday cupcakes still echoed through the house as sunlight poured through the windows, colorful flowerboxes spilled over on the porch, and a For Sale sign stood at the end of the driveway. Only eighteen months had passed since we'd moved into the rebuilt house. This was not our forever home. Deep down, I think we always knew that. The trauma of the fire was impossible to erase.

More insidious was the lingering sense that we didn't belong here—a low buzz of unease, a constant reminder that we weren't welcome, that we didn't quite fit in, that this kind of homogenous suburban life wasn't really ours. I recognized the shape of the feeling from childhood, yet this version unsettled me in ways I didn't yet understand. I tried to ignore it, but the unease lingered, even as I began to feel steadier.

Acupuncture and yoga had strengthened my nervous system, creating space for healing. I was glad to feel mentally stronger, more grounded. Present enough to grasp that while I had come a long way, I still had work to do. Healing is not the same as resolution. The underlying rupture in my narrative remained unrepaired. The story I had long told myself about who I was, what gave my life meaning, and where I was going remained incomplete. My identity was still fragmented.

I was no longer in crisis. But I didn't know what came next. Nothing felt quite right, not the neighborhood, not my job, not even my own skin. I had glimpses of normalcy, happiness, but they often lingered in my periphery, just out of reach. I wondered if this was an inevitable consequence of early menopause. I was several years postmenopausal, my essential hormones depleted. Was this what postmenopause felt like—lingering perpetually in a liminal state?

The consulting job was going reasonably well. I enjoyed leading the practice area at the boutique firm. It was a small company—just a handful of employees, fewer than had been on my HR team in my last role. The work was challenging but not demanding in the ways I was used to. Mostly, that was okay. But often, I felt like I was wearing a slightly too-tight pair of pants—not tight enough for anyone else to notice, but tight enough that I had to keep shifting in my seat, never quite at ease.

Gone were the grueling days and the intellectual thrill of a high-stakes financial technology company. Gone was the travel, the late nights at the bar, and the big paycheck. The tradeoffs were more time at home, more time on my yoga mat, more time with

Ken and Allison. I had loosened my tight grip on my professional identity.

I enjoyed the pace and culture. But still—it didn't fit. Or, more accurately, I didn't fit. The story I was trying to live wasn't congruent with the one deeply embedded in my consciousness from an early age. Try as I might, I was only one wrong move away from splitting my metaphorical pair of pants wide open. And then what? What would I do once I had to admit this job wasn't enough for me? I didn't have an answer.

One day while I was at lunch with a close colleague, my phone buzzed with a missed call from my mom. I hadn't noticed it come in. It had gone straight to voicemail. She was old-fashioned and would never call me while I was at work unless it was important. I excused myself and stepped away to listen. Her message was short, her voice calm. My dad had been taken to the hospital by ambulance. She didn't share any other details.

In the last decade, my relationship with my family had settled into a delicate equilibrium. The disappointment following my divorce, and my own need to be seen, had given way to a familiar rhythm of holidays, birthdays, and celebrations that resembled intimacy more than reality. The arrival of my niece and nephews pulled me back toward the kind of closeness I'd grown up with and wanted Allison to know. I no longer needed to matter in the way I once had and kept a measured distance most days. Yet the sense of being loved I'd carried since childhood remained—loved, not seen—steady, normal, and unspoken.

I tried calling my mom back, but she didn't answer. I returned to the table and continued chatting with my colleague, telling myself there was no need for concern.

Then my phone rang again—this time, it was my younger sister.

I answered quickly and stepped outside.

"Dad's gone," she said.

"Gone? What do you mean? Mom left a message that he was taken to the hospital . . ."

"Yes," she said. "But now he's gone."

I stood there, confused. "I don't understand."

"He died, Susan. He died."

I was overcome with emotion—mostly shock. My dad hadn't been in great health, but still. . . . He was dead. He was seventy-nine.

I returned to the table, both the waitress and my colleague looking at me with concern. I was ashen.

The waitress asked if I was okay. I shook my head, barely able to speak, holding back tears. "No, no, I am definitely not okay. My dad just died."

I hurried to my car and headed to the house in Somerville where I grew up, where my parents had lived for more than fifty years. It seemed impossible that I would never see my dad alive again. I thought about our conversations over the last several months. He had softened with age.

The bluntness that had defined him had dulled. He adored Allison, had a begrudging admiration for Ken, and trusted me to handle his final wishes. We had found a quiet peace in our relationship. His trust in those final months reminded me of the rare times I'd felt seen by him—brief flashes of affirmation I spent much of my life trying to recreate.

He was preparing for his death, getting his paperwork in order, reminding me of his last wishes. My dad was ready to die.

I knew it, even expected it, but not this soon, without warning, without time to say goodbye. But he died as he lived, on his terms, quietly and with dignity. He always said the only way he'd leave the Somerville house was in a box. In the end, it was a stretcher—but close enough.

I gave his eulogy. I don't remember much of it except the opening line: "What you saw was what you got with my dad—never one for pretense. He wasn't always the easiest, but he was real, authentic, and loved by many, especially his seven grandchildren."

My dad's sudden death interrupted my healing. His absence left an ache that surprised me. Grief and acceptance moved uneasily through me. I had been in the midst of trying to reclaim the throughline of my story after years of living in a splintered narrative—and now this. The ground moved again. The progress I had made suddenly felt blurry, out of reach, tenuous. New enough that it could slip away, that I could slip away.

In the months that followed, I was once again grieving what was gone while straining to see what might come next. My father's death had obscured the path I thought I was on. I was back standing in the unknown, suspended in time, full of doubt, surrounded by fractured images of myself that I couldn't piece together—what psychologists call possible selves, the imagined identities we hold about who we might become, who we hope to be, and who we fear we may turn into.[27]

[27] Hazel Markus and Paula Nurius, "Possible Selves," *American Psychologist* 41, no. 9 (1986): 954.

This perspective offered a way forward, a reminder that uncertainty also holds possibility. Yet it wasn't curiosity that propelled me. It was fear. Fear of failing again if I returned to the C-suite. Fear of choosing wrong, of getting stuck. Would consulting fulfill my professional ambitions? Would returning to school? Becoming a Pilates instructor? Immersing myself in nonprofit work? Each option held a different possibility, yet none offered clarity or confirmation.

How would I find my future self? By trying on different roles—like clothes in a fitting room—searching for the one that fit best? Or the one I liked most? I had no idea. But over the next few years, my life became something like a department store fitting room—trying new things, discarding them when they didn't fit, wondering if anything ever truly would.

As I searched for an identity that fit, our family was also beginning something new—we were moving again.

The house had sold quickly, and we bought a fixer-upper on the opposite side of town. We didn't want to disrupt Allison with another change in schools. Unlike Ken and me, Alli had put down roots in this town. She was thriving—doing well in school and socially. We moved as far from the scene of the fire as we could while staying within town lines. The new neighborhood was older and more established. The houses were set farther apart, with big yards and tall trees. It had a settled feel I hoped might be contagious. I wanted to feel settled. Maybe this would be our forever home.

Our newfound comfort in the ordinary made the move easy. The house was nothing special—small but welcoming. We were continuing our journey of simplifying, prioritizing peace and ease, and the transition to our new address unfolded without much hassle. No longer connecting our identities to our house made moving again transactional, not emotional. Particularly since the rebuilt house never felt like home.

In parallel with our move, Ken made a significant shift, taking a personal step to find ease by leaving behind his long career as a director of information technology to become a crew member at Trader Joe's. The politics of corporate America had never suited him, and he was craving less responsibility, less stress, and more space to breathe.

It was a big move, and not without consequence. The financial implications were real, though downsizing our home made the transition feel manageable. Beneath the change, there was also relief. We were both shedding identities that no longer fit. For Ken, the hierarchy and bureaucracy that had been suffocating him. For me, the illusion that my self-worth was tied to my job and my house. His decision didn't just happen beside mine. It was a recognition that he too could try something new and we would still be okay.

Ken's shift to Trader Joe's was effortless, as though he had been heading there all along. He walked away from status, pay, and responsibility without fuss, trading them for the simple rhythm of stocking shelves and unloading trucks. My struggle with who I was and who I might become continued. I longed for his ease, his confidence that he had made the right decision. His certainty only magnified my uncertainty. Where he sought less, I kept searching for more.

It was an unsettled time—the sadness of my father's death never far from the surface, Ken's new schedule reshaping our days, and another move still fresh. But we were no strangers to upheaval. If anything, change had become its own kind of stability. It felt like the right moment to step into a new opportunity, a way to reconnect with a piece of my former self.

After almost four years at the consulting firm, I was moving back to a corporate role, back to a Fortune 500 company. But not fully, not in my previous capacity. The role was several levels below the C-suite, an individual contributor in a specialized domain. It brought back the familiar rhythms of corporate life, but I didn't have to inhabit the entirety of my old professional identity. Could I partially inhabit a piece of my old identity? Would this satisfy my pursuit of a coherent narrative?

The answer became clear pretty quickly. No, I couldn't. Or at least not in this role and not at this company. I had virtually no authority, autonomy, or influence. It was dreadful. But for the moment, I was constrained—by timing, by circumstance, and by the reality of our new financial landscape.

I tried to make the job tolerable by pursuing growth in other areas and seeking challenges and stimulation outside of work. It became less about a singular possible self and more about experimenting with multiple selves, a concept rooted in self-development theory that embraces the fluid and evolving nature of identity.[28]

By trying on many selves, I hoped to preserve continuity in the piece of my professional identity that I had reclaimed, while expanding the possibilities of who I might become. Like changing

[28] Markus and Nurius, "Possible Selves."

out shoes or jewelry to give an outfit a different feel, not a complete reinvention, but an extension of the foundation.

Despite my best efforts, these selves didn't arrive in a neat, sequential order. They overlapped, collided, and often competed for my attention. I didn't leave one behind before stepping into the next. I toggled between them, layering roles in search of wholeness. Some lasted only a short time, while others stayed with me.

They weren't fully formed identities but fragments I tried on, tested, kept, or discarded—teacher, learner, guide, seeker. Each represented a different way of exploring purpose, learning, mindfulness, and healing. None stood alone, yet together they became the raw material for a new narrative. The pieces I was slowly stitching into a future self.

It reminds me now of the blankets my grandmother used to make, rows of small, crocheted squares, like quilts crafted from scraps and saved cloth. She would nimbly produce square after square, setting some aside for future use and discarding others altogether. And eventually, she would stitch them into something whole, something warm, durable, and cherished, passed down for years to come. A story made visible, square by square.

Alongside the piece of my professional identity that I had reclaimed, three distinct identities began to emerge, each speaking to a different part of me.

The first revolved around embodied healing. Mind–body work had been central to my well-being in recent years, and extending that focus felt natural. I added Pilates to my repertoire. It helped me feel stronger physically, reinforcing the confidence, sense of balance, and peace that yoga and acupuncture had helped me cultivate. I fell in love with it—its structure, its precision, its restorative potential. I decided to become an instructor, diving deep into anatomy and technique. Pilates is more technical than yoga, and its discipline appealed to me.

I was learning again—activating a part of myself that had long been dormant yet had been essential to my self-concept. I loved to learn. Yet, once I began teaching Pilates, I again felt like I was wearing something that didn't quite fit. I had tried on something that seemed like it should work but it didn't. It lacked depth, direction, and, most of all, purpose. I wasn't helping anyone heal. I was leading them through movement. The joy I'd felt in learning how to teach didn't translate into meaning when I taught. Quite the opposite, it didn't bring me energy. It drained it, which I could scarcely afford. I discarded teaching Pilates quickly.

It felt like another failure, yet in the effort—the learning, the teaching—I uncovered something essential. My job as a chief people officer had never been my purpose. That had been ambition, what had propelled me, shaped me, and, for years, sustained me. But I had mistaken ambition for purpose. To me, they had been indistinguishable.

Now, as I looked around the metaphorical fitting room at the roles I had tried on, I saw that purpose was not among the pieces. I had long regarded it as a luxury—available to others, but not to me, something only the truly privileged had the space to consider.

In the aftermath of so much upheaval, however, certain truths came into focus. One of them was my own privilege. It had been hard-earned—bootstrapped, even—but it was real. I had choices. I had an education. A roof over my head. Food on the table.

Privilege, I realized, was more basic than I had understood. It wasn't about money, the way I had always seen it. It was about opportunity, inclusion, freedom. As Kimberlé Crenshaw and other intersectional scholars remind us, privilege is never one-dimensional. It is shaped by overlapping layers of identity and experience.[29] In my constant striving to do more, be more, and achieve more, I had overlooked a simple truth. I wasn't lacking privilege. I was lacking purpose.

From this realization emerged a desire to give back, to share my privilege. I began volunteering with a nonprofit in Boston called Strong Women Strong Girls (SWSG). An organization empowering third- through fifth-grade girls in underserved communities to recognize their inner strength and pursue their dreams, supported by an incredible network of college mentors from six local universities.

I was hooked from the moment I heard one of the fifth graders share her dreams of going to college. The girls had just returned from a field trip to Harvard and were taking turns describing what they'd learned.

Mia, bold and bright-eyed, stood up and said, "I learned that I can go to college."

The group leader smiled. "Of course you can, Mia. But what helped you learn that today?"

Mia beamed. "All of the older kids at college have backpacks. And I do, too. So now I know I can go to college."

Her words stopped me. Not just for their innocence or clarity but because they touched me, reminding me of my younger self. The one who hadn't been entirely sure where she belonged or if

---

[29] Ahir Gopaldas, "Intersectionality 101," *Journal of Public Policy & Marketing* 32 (2013): 90–94.

she would go to college. My younger self, who was always hoping someone would notice me and say, "Of course, you can go to college, Susan. You can do whatever you want to. You matter."

That moment stayed with me. And so did the work. Over the years, I deepened my commitment, eventually serving on the board of SWSG for more than a decade, several of those years as board president. I went on to serve with other nonprofits, focusing on empowering girls and young women. Two decades later, this part of me—the one rooted in service, connection, and purpose—is no longer temporal. This self fit comfortably and became part of my emerging cohesive identity, a much more dimensional version than previous iterations. In many ways, it was what Erikson called generativity—finding meaning not only in my own growth, but in supporting the next generation.[30] This self wasn't temporary. It was part of me now.

A return to academics evolved next, stimulated by this exploration, learning things I didn't know, expanding my horizons beyond what had previously seemed possible. I thrived in school. It had fueled my sense of competence, starting in third grade with the infamous spelling bee. I'd returned to school in my early thirties for a master's degree, but it was perfunctory; I was checking a box, adding to my credentials to further fuel my career trajectory.

Now, in my late forties, I found myself toying with the idea of pursuing a PhD. A bold move for someone balancing a full-time job, a family, postmenopausal doldrums, and all of life's everyday responsibilities. It frankly seemed absurd. I didn't understand the first thing about becoming a PhD.

---

[30] Erikson, *Identity: Youth and Crisis.*

And then, out of the blue, after less than two years on the job, Trader Joe's offered Ken the opportunity to open a new store in Portland, Maine.

This was it, the chance for a proper restart.

We sold the house—another one that we never really loved, in the community that never quite felt like home—and moved to Maine. Allison was approaching seventh grade and, true to form, remained free-spirited and open to the adventure.

I quit the corporate job that had never quite fit. I enrolled full-time in a PhD program at Fielding Graduate University. I deepened my work with SWSG. And eventually, I found my way into a two-hundred-hour yoga teacher training program led by Rolf Gates.

More selves, yes—but I could feel a rising sense of coherence. I wasn't merely experimenting anymore. These pieces—purpose, learning, mindfulness, and healing—were beginning to come together. Not linearly, not neatly, but the way my grandmother's blankets had been stitched with care and intention. This was what I was building now—a life composed of meaningfully chosen squares. It was, I would later learn, the essence of post-traumatic growth—an identity reshaped not in spite of rupture, but through it.

But something was still unstitched.

I had been carrying grief from my father's death quietly, tucked away with other emotions I had yet to learn how to process, to integrate. With the move to Maine, I returned in earnest to my mat, to Rolf's teaching, and to the healing energy of yoga. I had come a long way, but I knew now that healing was not a destination.

Over the years, I often overlooked the complex interplay of physical, psychological, and social challenges that menopause presented. I knew better than most that menopause was not confined to disrupting my biology; it impacted every dimension of my life. It had changed how I saw myself, how I interacted with others, and how I navigated societal expectations. At times, the extent of my menopausal experience was eclipsed by the fire.

But it was always there, just beneath the surface.

Like identity itself, menopause is layered, evolving, and deeply personal. Looking at it with a biopsychosocial lens allows us to understand the profound interplay between our bodies, minds, and social worlds during this transition.[31] And just like identity is never static, menopause is not a singular story, not one person's story. It happens as part of a larger narrative of growth and change, offering unique opportunities to redefine who we are and how we show up in the world. Assuming we can survive the tumult, manage the symptoms, and figure out a path to integration.

I was approaching fifty, and with that milestone came a new determination. To rewrite my narrative and emerge anew, I needed to go deeper, to look at my menopausal experience holistically through this three-dimensional view. I had to reject my long-held story that stress and burnout had caused my departure from the C-suite, and only then had I coincidentally experienced early menopause. This wasn't the truth. It was a convenient excuse. They were not two isolated events. Severe onset

[31] Jane Kroger, *Identity Development: Adolescence through Adulthood*, 2nd ed. (Sage Publications, 2007).

perimenopause symptoms had dismantled my career, my sense of self, and my health.

I wanted to feel like myself again, not a muted version of the woman I had once been. The healing I had done had brought me a long way. But wholeness still eluded me. No amount of yoga or acupuncture could replace the hormones I had lost due to menopause. Nor could it protect me from further deterioration or the long-term health risks associated with hormone loss.

I needed medical intervention. I had to advocate for myself—stop accepting that nothing could be done or that this was simply normal aging. I had to reject the medical gaslighting. I didn't expect it to be easy, but I knew from months of research that without hormonal intervention, I was not likely to ever feel like myself again.

In the meantime, I had settled into the work of earning my PhD. I loved every minute of it—the research, the rigor, the conversations, the people. I was mentally alive in a way I hadn't been in years. Academics wasn't just another version of me or a possible path. It suited me. I felt at home in this space, curious, driven, and at ease.

My doctoral research focused on the connection between friendship and self-esteem in fourteen- to seventeen-year-old girls. The more time I spent supporting girls at SWSG, the more curious I became about what fosters confidence, self-efficacy, and resilience during critical adolescent years. This wasn't just theory. It was personal. And purposeful. It gave me a new language for understanding both the girls I was trying to empower and the girl I once had been—how my friendship with Mary had been shaping me for decades, long before I realized how central it was to who I became.

The findings were profound. The quality of close friendships is directly tied to how girls see themselves, their competence, and their worth. In other words, friendship isn't just companionship—it's identity. In writing that dissertation, I studied many girls, but in my heart, I was still writing about Mary and me. About how two awkward twelve-year-olds gave each other courage simply by believing in one another.

Friendship had not only shaped me personally—it became part of my scholarly lens, a way of understanding how we all construct our sense of self in the mirror of those who walk beside us. That lens was also shaping me: I had begun to integrate the many scattered pieces of myself—purpose, learning, healing. Yet my professional identity remained mostly on hold. Not the C-suite version of myself, polished and protective, but the softer, more authentic self I was yearning to claim. I couldn't imagine feeling truly whole without weaving my career back into my narrative.

But first, the crucial missing piece, the invisible, unspoken one—biology. I needed estrogen.

It was 2011. The Women's Health Initiative study from 2002 had cast a long shadow over hormone treatment for menopause, leading to widespread fear, confusion, and medical hesitation.[32] I was more than six years postmenopausal and considered outside the so-called window of safety for treatment. The barriers were steep, the data conflicting, and the stigma was real.

But I no longer felt powerless in the face of all the confusion. Adversity had given me strength. I could hold uncertainty, ask

---

[32] David H. Barlow, "Time to Reflect on the Women's Health Initiative (WHI) Study," *Human Reproduction* 18, no. 1 (2003).

better questions, and trust my instincts. I was determined and inquisitive. I was searching for more than answers. I was searching for liberation.

Liberation from the false story that stress and burnout had ended my career and menopause had merely followed. And from the collective resigned messaging that said, "Too bad. Now, all you can do is deal with it."

Dealing with it was no longer an option. I was desperate to fully reclaim myself.

With this renewed sense of agency, I made an appointment with a clinician at a hospital in Maine—an endocrinologist who claimed to be a menopause specialist. I was hopeful. Over the years, I had endured a wide range of menopausal symptoms, but the one bothering me most at this moment in time was a gradual weight gain of more than twenty pounds, concentrated in my abdominal area.

I had never carried weight in my midsection before. I knew the health risks associated with abdominal fat. After the fire, I had lost quite a bit of weight, so some gain was expected, even welcome. But now I felt like a stranger in my own body as the scale approached the same number as the one reflected when I was nine months pregnant with Allison, and a number far above what was typical for me most of my adult life.

A deeper concern was my mom's recent health decline due to osteoporosis. She was rapidly losing height and living with daily pain. Years earlier, Gram had died from complications following a hip fracture caused by the same disease. I was aware of the data on bone loss postmenopause and the genetic risks I carried.

But I never got to discuss any of these concerns with this doctor.

After a quick round of vitals, I sat waiting in the sterile exam room, clothed in a skimpy hospital johnny. When the doctor arrived, I explained my menopause status and concerns about sudden weight gain. He barely looked at me. "Well, you still seem pretty thin to me. Any other concerns?" That was it. Another dismissal. Another reminder of how easily women's concerns are brushed aside.

It echoed what I had endured years earlier in Boston: quick visits, no real listening, no help. After several more encounters just like it, I finally found something different—a clinic called Women to Women. It was cofounded by Dr. Christiane Northrup. I had picked up her book *The Wisdom of Menopause*, published in 2001, one of the few resources I could find explaining the importance of hormone therapy.[33]

It took a few months to get an appointment. The office was in a Victorian house on a side street in a quaint suburb. As I walked through the door, it had the same energy and promise of Huang Yu's office, the acupuncturist who had been instrumental in my healing journey. I knew I was in the right place. I would turn fifty in just a few weeks.

I was prescribed a fairly standard combination of estrogen and progesterone. The debilitating cognitive challenges I faced in perimenopause had settled as my hormone levels dwindled and my brain rewired accordingly. The physical and emotional symptoms I had been struggling with for the last few years were energy, mood, disrupted sleep, and weight gain.

---

[33] Christiane Northrup, *The Wisdom of Menopause: Creating Physical and Emotional Health and Healing During the Change*, 1st ed. (Bantam Books, 2001).

My hormone deficiency was so severe that I started to see improvements almost immediately upon beginning treatment. The feeling was familiar, like the first wave of relief I experienced after seeing Huang Yu. At that time, it was energetic and subtle, like something being unblocked. This time, it was targeted, cellular. But the effect was strikingly similar: Something long stuck had begun to move again. Tentative at first, then steadier, gaining momentum with each passing day.

There is no one-size-fits-all menopause and no one-size-fits-all path through it. Menopause before age forty-five is not that common, but for those of us in this category, hormone therapy is often not optional—it's critical. Biology had been my missing link. For all the psychological insight and spiritual healing I had undertaken, it wasn't until I addressed the physiological disruption caused by hormone deficiency that I could truly feel healthy again.

Healing isn't one-dimensional. The mind, the body, and the spirit don't heal in isolation—they are inseparably connected.

Many women describe menopause as a transformative stage marked by freedom, empowerment, and renewed clarity. Scholars and feminist thinkers, such as Germaine Greer and Jane Ussher, have written about postmenopause as a time of increased assertiveness, a loosening of external expectations, and a return to self.[34] Anthropologist Margaret Lock observed that in some cultures,

[34] Germaine Greer, *The Change: Women, Ageing and the Menopause* (Bloomsbury Publishing, 2018); Jane M. Ussher and Jane Ussher, *The Madness of Women: Myth and Experience* (Routledge, 2011).

menopause is seen not as a loss but as a transition into wisdom and social authority.[35]

These stories are compelling, and in sharp contrast to the biopsychosocial siege I had endured. The cultural silence, the dismissal from clinicians, and the internal gaslighting, had left me depleted, not empowered.

Our time in Maine was short—just one year—but in hindsight, it was essential. It gave me what I hadn't known I needed: space to explore, to slow down, and to begin integrating the fragmented selves I had accumulated along the way. Purpose. Learning. Healing. Was this the wisdom these feminist scholars write about?

I could viscerally sense an integration of these various selves, a coming together to articulate my rewritten narrative, stretching my post-traumatic growth further toward clarity, of where my life was going and how this learning would shape what came next. There was less of a sense of impermanence. These pieces were summoning lasting meaning.

When it came time to leave Maine, my exploration felt complete, at least for now. I had tried on many things, found the ones that fit, the ones that made me feel like me. They worked together, complemented each other, each a piece of a more substantive identity: complex, layered, dimensional.

We had planned to stay in Maine for several years, but that was not meant to be. As much as we loved Portland, the schools weren't a good fit for Allison. In Massachusetts, she had been an

---

[35] Margaret Lock, "The Politics of Mid-Life and Menopause," in *Knowledge, Power, and Practice: The Anthropology of Medicine in Everyday Life*, ed. Shirley Lindenbaum and Margaret Lock (University of California Press, 1993), 330–63.

average student who didn't try very hard. In Maine, she became an A student who didn't have to try at all. It felt like we were doing her a disservice by staying. So, we decided to return to where we had lived in Massachusetts before the fire, renting a place because we weren't ready to commit again.

We were going home—back to the town where we lived when we got married, where Allison was born, where we felt like we belonged. In that homecoming, I would begin reclaiming the missing piece of my narrative—my career. I was ready to lead again, shaped by everything I had been through. What once felt like fragments were becoming a cohesive self I could carry back into the world—stronger now, anchored in what mattered most.

Chapter 6

Reentry

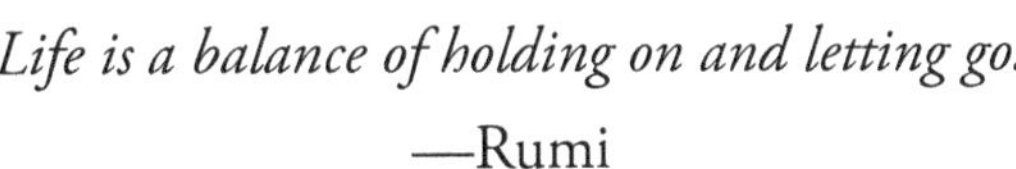

Life is a balance of holding on and letting go.
—Rumi

We were standing on yet another front lawn, looking at a house. This time, it was a small, nondescript rental property in the town where we lived before the fire. More than six years had passed since our house was destroyed by fire, and we were moving again, back to Massachusetts after a one-year hiatus in Portland, Maine. This was our third move in six years.

But this was more than a move back to Massachusetts; I was returning to a part of myself that I had been avoiding for some time. I was stepping back into the C-suite, to the chief people officer role I once held and loved so much.

It wasn't about reclaiming a title. I was testing whether I could weave my career back into the broader identity I had been piecing together these last several years. Could I step back into leadership and lead differently—shaped by the grace, care, and hard-won wisdom of those years away?

I never thought I'd go back. And in truth, you never really can. If I had learned anything since my resignation, it was that there is no such thing as going back.

Seven years had passed. Seven years of healing, learning, and growing. Seven years of trying to convince myself I was complete without an essential piece—one that had once defined me. My professional identity.

Yoga, doctoral studies, nonprofit work. I had expanded my sense of self beyond the narrow confines of a job while settling for professional roles that felt certain, controllable, and safe. Jobs that I couldn't fail at.

Self-doubt, anxiety, and confusion had clung to me since my resignation. I attributed much of it to menopause, and for a time, that was true. However, as hormone therapy restored my well-being and sense of self, I could no longer avoid the truth.

I was afraid. Afraid my past success had been luck, afraid I no longer measured up, and most of all afraid to fail. I couldn't name this as imposter syndrome at the time, but that's exactly what it was.[36] I didn't believe my success was fully mine. I feared one day that I would be exposed.

But things had shifted in the last several months. I was stronger, healthier, and ready to face my fears.

When the CEO of a technology startup called to ask if I would be interested in meeting for coffee to discuss the CPO role at his company, I said yes. Even though I'd been out of the

---

[36] Pauline Rose Clance and Maureen Ann O'Toole, "The Imposter Phenomenon: An Internal Barrier to Empowerment and Achievement," in *Women's Way of Knowing*, ed. Mary Field Belenky, Blythe McVicker Clinchy, Nancy Rule Goldberger, and Jill Mattuck Tarule (Basic Books, 1988).

C-suite for years, I still had a strong network in HR in the Boston area and a reputation as an executive who could balance strategy with execution—someone who could both roll up her sleeves and present to the board.

He had gotten my name from a friend and reached out directly to me. His timing aligned almost perfectly with our return to Boston. What struck me most was the fact that he wasn't deterred by the years I'd spent exploring. He saw them as additive, not a detour. The job required grit, and my nontraditional path made clear I had it. I accepted the role shortly after that meeting.

A month before I turned fifty, I hesitantly returned to the C-suite. It was unceremonious. No big announcement, no celebration, not even an updated headshot on the company website.

I had spent countless hours replaying the moment in the hotel conference room seven years earlier, the moment when I lost my train of thought, couldn't find my words, and fled in tears. In the intervening years, I let that meltdown define my entire career. I fixated not on the two decades of success that came before it but on how my competence had seemed to vanish in an instant as my erratic hormones destabilized my very foundation.

As I drove to work that first day, I was anxious but hopeful. This was a new beginning, a fresh start, a new chapter in my career. I felt a lightness and clarity—a sense that my career was no longer the whole of my identity, but one part of who I had become. This time, I wasn't there to climb, chase, or overperform.

I knew that this second chapter as a CPO wasn't about ambition. It was about showing up in alignment. No performance. No script. Just me.

I hesitated slightly as I walked into the office that sunny fall morning. The building was worn but welcoming. Inside, the space overflowed with people—sharing offices, the floor, the hallway. It was noisy, alive, brimming with scrappy, hardworking nerds.

It didn't have the pedigree I was accustomed to earlier in my career, but it felt infinitely relatable. Like Somerville. I fit right in. As Mary and I often joked, you can take the girl out of Somerville, but you can't take Somerville out of the girl. There would always be a scrappy, hardworking nerd inside me.

The environment made this CPO role feel safe—low risk. As did the anonymity. There was no team to disappoint, no one sneaking glances to see if I was stable, no colleagues wondering what might go wrong.

The only concern visible was mine when I looked in the mirror. Could I do this?

My mandate was to build a team that could scale the company for an initial public offering (IPO). It was challenging but doable, even while juggling my PhD and SWSG work. My capacity for work had returned to premenopause levels, but it felt different. Less urgent. And I was different. Less self-important.

It was hard to feel self-important when the dress code was jeans and a T-shirt. I shared an office with two other people, and I wasn't just leading the HR department; I *was* the HR department. Menopause and the fire had humbled me. And now, I was beginning to glimpse how that humility might shape the way I would lead this time.

I no longer had a parking space with my name on it, an executive assistant managing my calendar, or an unlimited expense account. Now it was jeans, T-shirts, and crowded desks. Like many things I had learned to live without, I didn't miss them. In yoga, aparigraha is the practice of loosening our grip—on possessions, dreams, plans, even people—because holding on too tightly to the past only leads to suffering.[37]

In every part of my life, I had been learning to loosen my grip—cultivating a mindset of enoughness and making space for what else might grow. How would all the work I had done serve me now? The healing through yoga. The PhD journey. The growth through trauma. This CPO role would not be shaped by ambition or future goals but by the wisdom gained through lived experience.

As I rolled up my sleeves and began the work I was hired to do, I remembered a Buddhist teaching "mindfulness is rooted in the heart, not the head."

I was now drawn to lead from a place of wisdom. Wisdom rooted in my heart, not committed to specific outcomes, or what might come next, but to what unfolded. Fully present, not striving, being. My edges had softened. My center had deepened.

I didn't need a step-by-step guide—just breath, the pause between action and inaction, and my values. This is what would guide my leadership now.

In the earlier chapter of my career, I was driven by performance, perfection, and the relentless need to prove myself. My leadership was tightly wound around goals, outcomes, and the unspoken belief that if I just worked harder, I'd be enough. It was polished, productive, and exhausting.

---

[37] Devi, *Secret Power of Yoga*, 174.

This time, my leadership—like my yoga—was a practice. A commitment to show up day after day. Sometimes strong and graceful. Sometimes unsure and unsteady.

The company had audacious goals, and my first task was to build a team that could scale quickly. But I built this team differently. I was drawn to more diverse candidates—not the kind of cookie-cutter high performers that I once aspired to be. It was more like assembling a puzzle: aligning people around their unique strengths to create a whole, rather than expecting each person to be whole unto themselves.

Through this approach, I became more aware of my own strengths and limitations in the context of the larger team. I could challenge and be challenged. I could admit mistakes and lean on others when I didn't have the answers. The relationships were transformative, not transactional. Success was no longer about individual performance, but about the strength of the collective.

My self-awareness had expanded, giving me an ease I hadn't possessed before. My shared office became a revolving door for teammates seeking a safe place to vent, to escape for a moment from the tensions inherent in working at a high-pressure startup.

Growth had taught me that my ambition and my purpose were not the same. They had so often felt interchangeable. But the satisfaction I found in my nonprofit work helped me realize that meaningful purpose was essential. It was no longer about being the best—but about helping others become their best. Enabling people to reach their potential became my purpose in this chapter of leadership.

One particular young man stands out. Fresh out of college, he brought entrepreneurial spirit, a fierce work ethic, and deep curiosity about the technical space we operated in. What he lacked in experience, he made up for with passion. I took a risk on him, as Carolyn had once taken on me. I invested time and energy in his development to help him achieve his goal of one day becoming a CPO. He did—well before his fortieth birthday.

The phrase *authentic leader* didn't resonate with me; it felt overused, hollow. What I craved was something more human—vulnerability. But vulnerability was messy, and I had generally avoided it most of my life, certainly at work. My mask of competence, composure, and performance had taken years to perfect. Revealing what was behind it wasn't easy, and I didn't always get it right. But I kept trying.

There's a delicate dance between openness and oversharing, honesty and seeking validation. I sometimes doubted myself outloud, not always successfully walking that fine line. With my vulnerability grounded in intention rather than attention-seeking, it created trust, invited connection, and made space for others to show up fully. What I came to understand was that leadership rooted in vulnerability could be steady, purposeful, and deeply human.

Leading in HR often means witnessing burnout, grief, failure, and self-doubt—my own and others. Compassion isn't about avoiding the hard stuff. It's staying human in the midst of it—listening, acknowledging, holding space with kindness and empathy. In yoga, as in leadership, discomfort is often where growth happens.

I learned to see compassion—for myself and others—as a leadership imperative. It increased my tolerance for imperfection, helping me see mistakes not as flaws but as teaching moments.

I became more adept at giving constructive feedback, helping others grow and gain confidence through support rather than criticism, and gently guiding them to see that learning comes from mistakes, not perfection. A lesson I wished I'd learned earlier.

My core values had always been grounded in integrity, but even core values can drift when we're tired, scared, or unsure. In those moments, it had sometimes felt easier to stay silent, to convince myself I could get comfortable with a decision that didn't fully align.

This time, when my values were tested, I didn't waver or seek the easy way out. I stayed in the discomfort and committed to aligning my words with my actions—and my actions with my values. Even when no one was watching. Especially then.

My leadership evolved alongside my academic work with an unexpected synergy. A PhD isn't just coursework. It is a process of becoming. It reshapes how you think and, ultimately, how you see the world and your place in it. My PhD journey became integral in rewriting my identity story and, with it, my identity as a leader.

Returning to the CPO role became more than a turning point in my narrative—it was a moment of integration. Leadership was no longer something separate from life experience. It was inextricably linked to it. My growth, my losses, my healing—each shaped how I would lead now.

Success for me looked different this time—slower, more reflective, rooted in humility and balance. I thought I had loved leading before—and maybe I did. But this kind of leadership? It didn't drain me. It gave me energy.

For a time, the company thrived, and so did I. But as often happens in startups, the growth outpaced the foundation, and cracks began to show. What once felt energizing soon turned chaotic, and the company began to fall apart.

It brought out a darker side of my boss, the CEO, which ultimately led to my resignation just before the company collapsed completely.

Nearly two years had passed since my hesitant first day. Layoffs were underway, funding had dried up, and the IPO we had once envisioned was no longer on the table. The stress in the executive team meetings was palpable.

When my boss asked to meet after one of those meetings, I didn't think anything of it. We often chatted informally throughout the day. But this time, he told me he planned to fire one of my colleagues. No warning. No merit.

I was aghast. I was no stranger to difficult decisions, but this one was unwarranted. He was looking for someone to blame, to be the scapegoat for the company's failure. I spent days trying to talk him out of it, citing reason after reason why it was ethically wrong. He wouldn't listen. And in the end, he fired him anyway.

I couldn't stay. Integrity had become more than a value—it was my internal guide. I resigned without hesitation.

He was angry. We never spoke again.

It was an unfortunate ending to my return to the C-suite, but I remain deeply grateful for the opportunity. The messy, chaotic nature of that company gave me the space to reenter leadership on my own terms—grounded, coherent, and sustained by inner wisdom.

I declared victory—with relief—and moved on to my next role.

I was roughly halfway through my PhD by this point, entering the phase of the program where you design your study and begin the ultimate deliverable: the dissertation. I needed a job that would allow me to balance these academic demands with raising a teenager while continuing to prioritize my well-being.

The next role offered that balance. For the next few years, I worked in a job I didn't love but genuinely liked. It gave me the stability I needed for my academic and personal life, while still offering professional momentum. A chance to integrate what I'd learned at the startup and lean again on the skills that had once made me a strong CPO. The firm was established, elite, privately held, and exceptionally well-funded—both a prestigious step up and a safe haven that allowed me to reestablish myself with my new rules firmly in place.

Even with that stability, the PhD stretched me further than I had anticipated. Becoming a PhD was far more than I had imagined at the start of the program. It had been a naïve decision, with the odds of success stacked against me. Fewer than 2 percent of adults in the US hold PhDs, and about half of those who begin doctoral programs don't finish.[38]

During the five years it took me to complete my degree, I often considered not finishing. My career was back on track; Allison was in high school, almost fifteen. We loved where

---

[38] Andy Stapleton, "How Many People Have PhDs? Number of People With Doctoral Degree," Academia Insider, August 27, 2024, https://academiainsider.com/how-many-people-have-phds/; "Attrition in Humanities Doctorate Programs," American Academy of Arts and Sciences, accessed August 27, 2025, https://www.amacad.org/humanities-indicators/higher-education/attrition-humanities-doctorate-programs.

we lived, and Ken's job at Trader Joe's was an excellent fit for his skills and disposition.

I didn't need a PhD to feel complete.

Yet the deeply independent and sustained pursuit of my research had a hold on me that was hard to put into words. It became part of mending my fractured identity, returning me to the self-authorship of my story, and shifting my sense of achievement from roles to meaning. It was also a testament to the discipline and resilience that, deep down, continued to drive me despite how much I had grown over the past decade.

My growth in relating to others had accelerated as I returned to leadership with less ambition and more compassion and vulnerability. My ability to connect in a profoundly human way was deeply fulfilling, but with my family as always, it was different. The old patterns lingered, and I sometimes wondered if I had changed at all. A part of me still longed for my mother's approval, still hoped she might see me differently one day.

In the years after my father died, my mother stayed independent and reasonably healthy. Our relationship remained what it had always been—pleasant, slightly distant, never quite as close as we might have been. She didn't understand my pursuit of a PhD, though she never said much about it. When I told her the end of my program was fast approaching and gave her the date of my final presentation, she agreed to come. She seemed more relieved than proud.

Twelve days before that day arrived, she died.

It was a Wednesday, and she hadn't been feeling well since the weekend when we'd attended my cousin's wedding. She'd been in great spirits that day—healthy, energetic. By midweek, she was short of breath and called an ambulance to be safe.

I visited her in the hospital after work on Thursday. She was alert, breathing okay, and annoyed with the doctors. They told her she had pneumonia; she was certain she did not. True to form, she was more irritated about being stuck in the hospital for the weekend than about being sick. The Patriots were playing, and she wanted to be home to watch the game. I left unconcerned, assuming she'd be back in her chair by Sunday, Tom Brady on the screen.

When I returned the next day, her breathing had worsened, but she was still lucid. Instead of complaining about when she was going to be released, she looked at me seriously and said, "Susan, I've had a good life. I have a blouse for you to put me in for a wake."

"Wait—what happened to watching the Patriots on Sunday?" I asked, startled.

"It's not pneumonia. It's my Barrett's," she said, referring to the condition she'd managed for years.

I deflected. "I thought you didn't want a wake—what's with the blouse?"

She smirked. "Your sister will never let you not have a wake." Then, with a twinkle: "But make sure I look good. If I don't, shut the casket immediately."

"Look good?" I asked, skeptically.

"You know what I mean," she said and asked to rest.

I left bewildered.

A few hours later, I got a call from the hospital. My mother had been moved to the ICU, and the doctor wanted to intubate her. But my mom had been explicit with me—her health care proxy—for months, years even: no intubation, no resuscitation.

I rushed to the hospital. My sisters and brother-in-law were already there. Before anyone could speak, I said, "No tube."

They stared at me—Ken included. My younger sister said, aghast, "You're just going to let her die?"

I was incredulous. "You know this is what she wants."

A doctor stood silently by, watching our standoff.

I asked to see my mother.

She was still conscious, but her breathing had worsened. I sat beside her.

"Mom," I said, "they want to put a tube in you. I said no."

She pulled off her oxygen mask and choked out a few words: "It's okay, Susan. I'm dying anyway. Don't make your sisters mad at you."

Mad at me? I was furious. The doctor intubated her.

The next day, a respiratory specialist confirmed what my mother had already known. She did not have pneumonia, or at least not in a traditional sense. She was suffocating. Her lungs were filling with fluid, her esophagus deteriorating, likely from the Barrett's. She would not recover. She was eighty-two.

Within hours, surrounded by family, the doctor removed the tube. It had been in for less than twenty-four hours. She died almost immediately after the tube came out. Peacefully breathing her last breath.

A few days later, I walked into the funeral home, telling my sisters to wait by the door. I was prepared to close the casket if she didn't look good.

But damn, she did. She looked like she was sleeping.

We celebrated her life exactly as she wanted. All the details were in the folder she'd labeled the "mom file." The prayers, the songs, the burial. My mother's attention to detail, her intelligence, and her strong personality never abandoned her. She was in charge until the very end.

It was hard to process that she was no longer in the world—a week earlier, she'd been dancing at my cousin's wedding.

Over time, I've come to appreciate the gift in the sudden deaths of both my parents, seven years apart. Not having to watch them suffer. Not having to care for them as their health slowly deteriorated or wonder when the final moment would come. There's a blessing in that.

And also, a longing. If only I had more time. I should have said more. I should have told her how brave she was—how amazed I was that they both met death without fear. More afraid of being a burden than of dying. More afraid of losing control over their last days than of letting go.

But grief was complicated for me. In general. And especially with my parents.

I had pushed away the grief of my dad's death for many months, not wanting to face another loss. And my relationship with him was far less complex than the one I had with my mom. I gave my dad more grace. Perhaps because so little had ever been expected of him. I didn't look to him for emotional understanding, and so his silence was forgiven, even excused.

When I was younger, I occasionally felt seen by him. I would sense that he understood I was different from my sisters. Sometimes I felt like I mattered to him.

But with my mom, feeling like I mattered remained elusive. And she bore the weight of my expectations. She was the mother.

Her love wasn't supposed to be earned. And it was her I blamed for my persistent feeling that I was never enough.

And now that she was gone, I was stuck—grieving not just her, but the dream that she would one day see me, get me, love me as much as she loved my sisters. The weight and the irony of her death pressed down on me. I had never felt truly seen by her and yet, in the end, wasn't that precisely what happened? The contradiction in those last hours of her life, the ache of invisibility alongside a fleeting sense of being seen, became one of my hardest truths.

Twelve days later, I defended my dissertation as scheduled. Of course I did. She wouldn't have wanted it any other way. I wasn't resilient and self-reliant by accident. My parents raised me that way—intentionally or not. I'll never know.

My mother's inability to see me in life mirrored the void I had tried to fill for years. Maybe being seen was never the point. But I had found a way to see myself. Becoming a PhD was mine alone. No one asked it of me. No one needed it from me. It was a commitment I made to myself and kept.

A different reflection now looked back at me in the mirror. Not the kaleidoscope of blurred images from that fateful day ten years earlier when I was sobbing on the floor of a hotel bathroom, alone and afraid. Now I saw someone whole and coherent. I had emerged from that period of disorientation and, in that moment in time, I felt complete.

Yet I had come to understand that wholeness, like identity, is never fixed. Things come together, they fall apart, and they come together again. That rhythm was no longer something I feared, but something I could live within. I had found a way to integrate the pieces of my growth, stitching them together like my grandmother's blanket.

My dissertation was on friendship, and yet I never anticipated that one of the greatest gifts of my doctoral work would be the friendships themselves. I graduated with a group of true friends—lifetime friends. There are six of us, spread out across the United States and Canada. We met on the first day of orientation and formed our own learning cohort. A bit of a phenomenon, really. Against all odds, we stayed together for the entire program—and every one of us became a PhD.

For the duration of our studies, and even for a time after, we emailed each other six days a week, each of us on an assigned day. It was life-giving, sustaining me at times when I thought I would never finish the long journey of becoming a PhD in human and organizational systems. More than that, we supported each other through all the ups and downs of life—family crises, loss of loved ones, health scares, and the sheer exhaustion of juggling graduate work with demanding careers.

These friendships were different from the ones forged in childhood or at work. They were built on shared understanding, mutual vulnerability, and unconditional support. We understood each other's ambitions and doubts, our passion for learning, and our fears.

In many ways, these friendships were as formative as my research itself. They expanded my understanding of what it means to belong—not through shared history, as with Mary, or through proximity, as with colleagues, but through a shared commitment to growth. They reminded me that friendship, at its core, is about being witnessed and believed in, no matter your age or stage.

Looking back, I realize that my doctoral friendships gave me something I didn't even know I needed: the sense that I was not alone in remaking myself.

When I walked across the stage a few months later, I could hear my friends, my cohort, cheering loudly. I could see Ken clapping. I could see Allison smiling. My niece Meghan grinning. My heart was full.

Just six months later, it was Allison's turn to walk across the stage and graduate from high school. Two graduations, two generations, back-to-back. Ken was clapping. I was smiling.

True to her independent spirit, Alli navigated high school with minimal fuss or drama. Not none—but not much. She was grounded, funny, and clear on who she was. She wasn't interested in sports and didn't chase extracurriculars for the sake of a resume. Instead, she picked up part-time jobs, paid for her gas, and enjoyed the freedom that came with it.

She was popular in a low-key, likable way and had a big, loud, lovely group of friends who laughed a lot and looked out for each other. She was eager for what came next—ready to leave home and head off to college.

We were excited for her. But as I watched her take those final steps across the stage, I couldn't help but see all of her at once. Memories flooding me with warmth and love.

The toddler who insisted her chocolate milk be heated twice—thirty seconds each time—listening closely for two dings of the microwave, inconsolable otherwise.

The ten-year-old who failed English because she didn't like the book—and when asked what she'd do differently, calmly replied, "I said I didn't like the book."

The teenager who couldn't wait to drive and skipped an English test to get her learner's permit, risking her final grade, so she could get behind the wheel as soon as her age allowed.

She had always known her own mind. As she crossed that stage, confident and clear, I knew we had done a good job. She had done an even better one. Watching her, I saw what it meant to raise not only a daughter but also myself. She had grown into her own, and in the self-assured way that she held herself, I glimpsed the continuation of the narrative I had so often struggled to author for myself.

She was ready for what was next. I was, too. Mostly.

It had been less than a year since my mom had died, and as I stood there watching Alli receive her diploma, I was half laughing, half crying at a memory.

Months earlier, Alli and I had taken Mom to lunch for her eighty-second birthday. At one point, she paused and said, "I don't think I'll make it to my next birthday."

"Oh, Grammy," Alli groaned, "that is so morbid. What about my high school graduation?"

My mother, without missing a beat, said, "Oh, honey, I've been to a lot of high school graduations."

And that was that.

For the last decade, life had felt like a series of thresholds—one door closing, another not quite open. Sometimes, I passed through quickly. Other times, I stood in the hallway, frozen in that liminal space, waiting far longer than I wanted to.

But now, finally, everything had landed. The doors behind me had quietly shut. The questions I once carried were either resolved or released. For the first time in years, I wasn't hovering between what was and what might be. I was moving forward—with both feet under me.

Ken and I bought a condo in Boston. We were putting down roots again—this time as empty nesters. Strange, but exciting.

My parents were gone, but their spirits and memories remained close. For a time, I assumed the role they never explicitly named but seemed to have reserved for me. I had spent a lifetime trying to fit in, to belong. And now, I felt implicitly tasked with not just belonging, but leading, playing the connector role that had been my mother's, gathering everyone for holidays, upholding the family traditions, trying my best to keep in touch. The irony wasn't lost on me.

It was a bit disorienting, yet I remained grounded, steadier, not just in my family, but in myself.

This sturdier version of me was ready to step into something bigger, more purposeful, a position that would enable me to make the impact I had been on the precipice of when my career was derailed.

Several months earlier, I'd received a phone call from a recruiter about a chief people officer role at a growing life sciences company in Cambridge. In the midst of the many things swirling about, I said, "No thanks" and didn't think about it again. Then they called back.

The job was still open. Did I want to interview? The CEO wanted to meet me. I smiled; this could be a once-in-a-lifetime opportunity. So much had changed in just a few short months. I was ready. I scheduled the interview.

Redemption, I had learned, was not a destination. Like wholeness, it was never fixed. Things come together, they fall apart, and they come together again. Like leadership, like yoga, like life itself, redemption is a practice.

Chapter 7

Integration

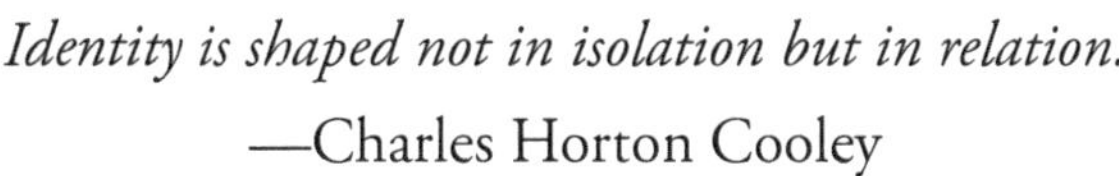

Identity is shaped not in isolation but in relation.
—Charles Horton Cooley

The Boston skyline blurred past the dirty train window. I was headed to interview for the chief people officer role at a fast-growing life sciences company with a mission to transform cancer care. As I gazed out the window, I thought about how I had changed since returning to the C-suite several years earlier. Changes that gave me an understated confidence that this job was mine before I stepped into the company's headquarters.

As the train rumbled over the bridge into Cambridge, I reflected on how I felt when I accepted my first CPO role all those years ago. I never doubted whether I should be at that table or not. I earned my seat through hard work, competence, and confidence. A culmination of twenty years of dedication to a career that I loved. Now here I was again, more than a decade later, my meandering path leading me to an opportunity that would require me to show up fearlessly, without pretending, without performing, without compromising. A job where I could bring my whole self, even the broken, chipped, and dented pieces. The days of questioning my capabilities, fearing failure, or playing small were gone.

The lobby shimmered in the sunlight as I sat waiting to meet the CEO. The space was immaculate, a modern mix of laboratories and offices, polished brightly in service to the vital work the company did each day supporting cancer patients. The space hummed with energy, vibrating with purpose, urgency, and care.

My confidence increased. I could feel it in my bones. I was meant to be here. My skills, perseverance, and desire to make a difference in the world—not just in my career—had brought me here, to a company that valued saving lives more than its Wall Street valuation. It just made sense, like the days when I gracefully stepped into and held the peak pose in yoga practice, with no wiggles, no wobbles. I had this.

And I did. I got the job. The CEO and I clicked immediately. He is a quirky, intelligent, and mission-driven guy who began his career selling copy machines. He cares deeply about the patients, the work, and the employees. My nonlinear path to his office didn't faze him in the slightest. He wasn't looking for a predictable HR executive with years of biotech experience. He was looking for someone with determination, brains, and heart. Someone he could trust to help him fulfill the company's mission.

I was that person. It took a few months to complete the formal process and meet all the right people. My confidence wavered from time to time as the bureaucracy dragged on, the hurrying up to wait for the next step. But eventually, the offer letter arrived. I was ecstatic. I gave my notice at the financial services firm; it had been a meaningful step along my path to this new role. I cherish the relationships I made there, the strong team I was privileged to build and lead, and the lessons I learned. It may not have been the job of a lifetime, but it was a chapter I was thankful for.

It was late summer when I started the new job. I walked to catch the train on my first day. The station was just a few blocks from our new condo. I found myself once again gazing out the dirty windows at the blurry Boston skyline, but this time I wasn't reflecting on the past, on what had brought me here. I was anticipating the future, the excitement of joining the leadership team of this prestigious life sciences company. I had an innate sense of belonging, a feeling that often eluded me, but it had somehow settled in my psyche. I would belong here, be part of something, matter. I was pulsing with excitement about expanding and leading the HR team, which at this company was called the People Team.

I had not even attended orientation yet, but I already hoped this would be my last full-time position as a CPO. I was fifty-five and was manifesting an exhilarating seven- to ten-year period where I would be challenged, stretched, and called on to deliver the best performance of my career.

And for a time, it was precisely that—a career dream come true.

When I arrived at the office that first day, it was without pretense; it was like stepping onto my mat, pausing, breathing, and simply arriving. And what followed was natural, rhythmic. It flowed, like a well-paced vinyasa class, one move after the next.

The CEO and I met to discuss his goals for HR. We chatted easily as he jotted down the priorities on the whiteboard. I still remember them. Strengthen and build the team. Bring down turnover. Ensure high employee engagement. Meet our hiring plans. Return to Boston's Best Places to Work list.

As we wrapped up our first of many meetings, he gently challenged me to complete these priorities and be ready for a new set in ninety days. I loved a challenge. I left his office, rolled up my sleeves, and got to work.

It wasn't easy; in fact, the pace was relentless. It sometimes felt like we were trying to transform cancer care with bubblegum and Band-Aids. I spent hours in one-on-ones, mainly listening to what wasn't being said, balancing the need for everyone to feel heard with the need to move quickly. Ninety days didn't seem like much time, but our mission could not wait. Bold, decisive action was required to meet the company's aggressive deadlines.

This tension—between urgency and care—was impossible to ignore. Restructuring the team in those early days, even after decades in HR, was hard. The voice of my first mentor often whispered in my ear, "If it ever gets easy, it is probably time to move on." They never did, and this restructuring was no exception. It was particularly challenging. There were no obvious jerks, underperformers, or visible incompetence, yet the team was struggling, not meeting its goals, and lacking integration.

I quickly assessed that the team's structure—too many levels, decision-making concentrated with too few people, role confusion—was impeding its ability to execute effectively and slowing things down. Getting it right required changing some roles, letting one person go, and hiring several new people.

I relied on the instincts I had refined since returning to leadership. Difficult conversations and decisions that once felt daunting were far less so when I led with my heart, balanced by listening and honesty. I was able to align everyone with the changes, even the one person I had to let go.

She called me several months later and asked to meet for coffee. She wanted to thank me. She shared that letting her go was the best thing that I could have done for her. She was in the wrong role and knew it, struggling in silence, because she couldn't bear the thought of leaving. Boy, could I relate.

This difficult decision, along with the many that followed, strengthened my evolution from a performative, competent leader to one whose identity had moved beyond traits and behaviors, embracing the interconnectedness that comes with being a leader. A leader who nurtures those around her to be human by being human herself. Leadership at its best is a highly involved role, often undifferentiated from self.[39] For reasons I didn't fully understand, it had taken me some time to see leadership as an essential part of my self-concept. Part of who I am versus something that I did—integrated as part of my identity, not distinct.

It seemed like my ability to lead was finally self-actualized—Maslow's highest need—but for me it wasn't about achievement; it was about alignment. I released ego, success, and effort as measures of effectiveness in exchange for leading through my values and principles. This alignment created an ease in this role that was often hidden under a massive pile of tasks.

Yet, it was visible in the success of the team I led. They thrived—not only as individuals, but together, as a collective.

---

[39] Boas Shamir et al., "Leading by Biography: Towards a Life-Story Approach to the Study of Leadership," *Leadership* 1, no. 1 (2005): 13–29.

I have a photo of that early team framed on my desk, everyone smiling brightly in aprons and chef hats at a rustic Italian restaurant where we'd spent the afternoon preparing dinner together. Joy radiates from the photo.

When I look at it, I see not just their smiles, but my own—my identity as a leader fully realized, proof that I could nurture and be nurtured at the same time. This team went on to do amazing work, their delight fueling our results as much as any strategy or plan. Their alignment showed up not just in moments like that photo, but in the work itself.

Ninety days passed in the blink of an eye. The CEO and I met again in his office; the list of my priorities had faded but was still visible on his whiteboard. Turnover was trending downward, hiring metrics were promising, and the HR team had been reorganized. Engagement would take more time, but we hit our goals and landed back on the Best Places to Work list before my first anniversary.

The CEO was delighted with the progress. The company was well-positioned for what was ahead. I thought I was, too.

Allison was doing great at a small private university in the Boston suburbs. Ken and I loved living in the city. Commuting by train each day to Cambridge brought back fond memories of my daily trek to UMass Boston years earlier. My days had been long then and were just as long now, sometimes longer. There was comfort in the routine, but more than that, I had purpose, relationships, and freedom to do my best work. It was motivating, almost to the point of intoxication, yet my well-being remained intact.

I settled into that sense of connection that had drawn me to this position a year or so earlier. I started to envision, and even plan, retiring from this job. It had been years since I felt so grounded, clear, and capable.

And then, unexpectedly, I lost a long-standing friendship, one that I thought would last forever. Nearly twenty years of shared history disappeared in what felt like an instant. The reasons she gave didn't ring true—perhaps to protect me, perhaps to protect herself. At this point, the specifics no longer matter. What mattered was the grief. I was heartbroken.

That loss gave me pause. I had written an entire dissertation on the power of friendships to shape identity, and my own life was a testament to that truth—Mary, my doctoral cohort, the friends who had carried me through rupture and loss. But this ending reminded me of something else. Identity is never fixed, never finally done. Belonging can feel steady, until it isn't. I had mistaken wholeness for connection, for a sense of completion that depended on being seen. Losing it reminded me that wholeness was never something to be secured, only something to be returned to.

It was a reminder that the path itself is the work. Identity isn't about reaching some state of permanent arrival. It's about learning to integrate what is, and what is no longer, into the self you carry forward.

I didn't realize how soon that lesson would return in another form. About eighteen months into my tenure, small changes began at work—slight at first, easy to dismiss, until suddenly they could not be ignored.

I knew from the beginning that the company could be a target for acquisition. In the life sciences sector, it is common, especially when a majority shareholder is one of the world's largest pharmaceutical companies. But that possibility never factored into my decision to join. I wasn't chasing an exit. I was drawn to the role for reasons that ran deeper, and my motivation grew stronger each day, one success at a time.

Near year's end, as we prepared for the fourth quarter board meeting, anxiety was high. The rumors were true. The company was being acquired in an all-cash deal. I should have been excited. The equity tied to my role was meaningful. The company would receive the financial infusion it needed to accelerate our mission. Many small biotechs never realize this kind of success. We did.

It was a big deal. I wasn't excited. I was sad.

I knew things would change. I didn't know what or how fast, but I knew that whatever came next would not be the same. I hoped things would unfold slowly, giving me time to acclimate. But that was not the case. After the board meeting, the chairman asked to meet privately. I sighed. Here we go. I had a pleasant relationship with him, but we rarely met one-on-one. I knew this was important.

He got right to the point. The new owner would be replacing the CEO in the coming weeks. My boss. My friend. Ugh. He asked me to meet with the incoming CEO and begin confidential transition planning. I felt sick. Yes, it was part of my job—the absolute worst part. I valued our CEO's counsel and support. I'd grown accustomed to his quirks. I enjoyed working with and for him. I hated keeping a secret from him.

As I walked back to my office from the boardroom, all I could think was *buckle up*. Change was coming, fast and furious. I took a deep breath and shut my office door.

A few days later, I met the new CEO over video. She said all the right things. I was hopeful.

In the meantime, my boss seemed unaware he would soon be leaving. I avoided him as much as possible, until one day, he dropped in and sat down across from me.

"I think I'm being replaced," he said.

Shit. Now what do I say?

I couldn't lie—not to him. So, I asked, "What makes you think that?"

Good thing it wasn't my first rodeo.

He explained that the board chair had asked to meet with him the next day. Rumors were flying at the parent company. But more than that, he said, it was instinct.

So again, I deflected. "How do you feel about that, if it's true?"

He seemed conflicted, hesitant as he considered my question. His payout was life-changing. He could retire or serve on boards. But he loved his job. He loved the company.

I nodded. I understood.

We sat in silence for what felt like an eternity. Then he left. A single tear streamed down my cheek. I straightened my shoulders and took a deep breath.

There was a company meeting the next day. The CEO's departure was announced. He took the stage, upbeat, proud of the company's accomplishments, and excited about the future. I clapped, smiled, and hoped for the best.

He never asked whether I knew. I assume he knew I did. Neither of us wanted it to affect our relationship.

The hand-off was swift. Within weeks of the sale, my old boss was gone. The new CEO took his seat at the conference room table, moved into his office, and even assumed his executive assistant as her own.

I knew from experience. Change waits for no one. I shook off my trepidation and got back to work. The influx of funding enabled the expansion of the HR team, adding much-needed expertise and implementing the most aggressive hiring plan we'd seen to date.

Daunting—but if any team could do it, it was this one. As we turned the calendar to the new year, we hit the ground running.

But we were barely back from holiday break when the tide turned.

Many of my executive colleagues had clauses in their contracts that enabled them to trigger their exits, collect their payouts, and walk away. One by one, they came to see me, to let me know and ask for help. They had their reasons. By fall, most of the executive team I had joined was gone–many of them having chosen to leave on their own terms, others having been asked to leave by the CEO. By year's end, only one colleague and I remained from the original team.

It felt like a different place. But the mission was the same and it still mattered. I clung tightly to the idea that I would retire from this job. Yet with each departure, a piece of me left with them. I could feel the coherence of my narrative fraying. The team I had joined was gone, and with it, the ease and acceptance I had once felt.

I was one of two executives who received a retention package; mine would have kept me there for several years. But that wasn't the point, I wanted to stay, even as I felt my place on the executive team subtly shifting. I am not sure exactly when it happened, but the dynamic had changed, and I was slipping to the outside of the circle I once stood firmly within.

What had once been a positive, even friendly relationship with the CEO became strained. Uneasy. It was as if, now that most of her leadership team members were people she had chosen, my value had diminished. It was understated, but real.

In late January 2020, I met with my executive team colleagues to review proposed changes to the HR team's structure. The team had grown significantly the previous year and had become a bit unwieldy. The generous budgets typical of the first year after an acquisition were tightening, and I needed to cut some costs—meaning people—to make everything work.

The review went well. I got their blessing to move forward and executed the changes. Shortly after the changes had been announced, during our weekly one-on-one, the CEO and I were discussing the restructuring when she asked, "So what about you?"

I replied, "What about me? It's my team—I plan to continue to lead it."

She murmured something vague, but unmistakable: she thought it might be time for me to leave.

"Are you firing me?" I asked, incredulously.

She backpedaled, saying she was just wondering what it would cost for me to leave—in other words, for her to package me out, like the ten or so executives who had exited the prior year.

This job was priceless to me, and the suggestion left me speechless and infuriated.

But more than that, I was hurt. I felt betrayed. Like a middle schooler whose best friend has just decided she doesn't want to be friends with her anymore. Or the adult realizing that a relationship she once trusted has quietly shifted. Unsettled. Unmoored.

In early February, she presented me with a package to leave that summer, with the announcement planned for April. I was perplexed. My performance had been outstanding. The HR team had the highest engagement scores in the company. We had met or exceeded every goal the year before. The same team whose happiness I see in the photo on my desk—aprons, chef hats, laughter. They had done amazing work. How could that not count? How could I not count?

I didn't want to accept the package. But I no longer trusted her. Staying felt as impossible as leaving. I signed the agreement and accepted the reality that I would not be retiring from this company.

I never got an explanation.

In spite of decades in HR, it had never occurred to me that I wouldn't leave this job on my own terms. I had never been fired from anything—not a retail job, not even a newspaper route. It was disorienting.

And the disorientation was only beginning.

Two weeks after signing the transition package I didn't want, we sent employees home as the COVID-19 pandemic shuttered businesses—at first, we thought, for just two weeks.

I hadn't experienced this kind of professional chaos since the turmoil following September 11, when life as we knew it was suddenly upended. Like that time, the HR team would be central in navigating the upheaval, keeping employees safe, informed, and cared for. I had to step up and lead, even though I was still reeling from my termination. Firing. Transition. Call it what you will. I didn't know what to call it.

What I did know was that regardless of the circumstances, this ending would not be my ending.

There was very little I couldn't survive. I had already lost my first career, my health, our house, and both my parents. And while survival had sometimes felt like the best I could manage on the hardest days, the truth was I had done more than survive. I had grown. I was wiser, stronger, and more grounded.

I had thought this job was it, the final piece of the puzzle, the rewritten last chapter in the story of a career that had not unfolded as planned.

Redemption.

I guess it was, until it wasn't. Life is funny that way.

The chaos of the pandemic delayed my departure. The CEO and I reached an uneasy agreement: I would stay through the end of the year, and no announcement would be made until early fall. Only a handful of people knew I was leaving and that it wasn't my choice. The secret would hold for months.

I stayed because I believed in the team, the people, and the mission—and in showing up when it mattered, no matter the circumstances. I did my best to lead with grace. Some days were easier than others.

The busyness of those early pandemic months was a convenient distraction from the inevitability of my exit. It was easy to forget that day was coming. It was easier still not to think about it at all. I was grieving again, grieving the loss of this job, while performing a role that I had been written out of.

I was back in a liminal space, floating between two worlds, hovering between two identities. The one I was and the one I would become. Narrative identity theory suggests we make meaning of ruptures by threading them into our life story.[40] In this rift, I wasn't only in transition between roles. I was revising my understanding of who I was.

The difference this time was that I recognized this space, the in-between. I understood what it felt like. I knew how to navigate it, grow through it, and learn from it. Or at least I thought I did.

And I still hated it, knowing I was leaving, pretending I wasn't. Eventually, this disruption would settle into something more permanent—the time "before I was fired," adding one more "before" to my list. Before menopause derailed my career. Before the fire brought me to my knees. Before I returned to the C-suite. Before my parents died.

Some identity theorists describe these moments as transitions between selves—spaces where the old self no longer fits, and the new one has yet to take form. As Erikson argued, identity is never fixed. It is revised and reshaped across our lives.[41] I had lived through enough ruptures, perhaps more than most, that I understood this and also knew I wasn't alone. Illness, loss, divorce, caregiving, motherhood—we all move through these invisible transitions. Our identities unraveling and reassembling

---

[40] Dan P. McAdams, "Narrative Identity: What Is It? What Does It Do? How Do You Measure It?" *Imagination, Cognition and Personality* 37, no. 3 (2018): 359–72, https://doi.org/10.1177/0276236618756704.

[41] Kroger, *Identity Development: Adolescence Adulthood.*

in ways the world may never see. Sometimes, we can't even see it ourselves.

But this time, I could see it. Unlike most of my "befores," this one didn't take me by surprise. It was clear, unavoidable, and growing closer as each day passed, and the end of 2020 drew near.

The CEO announced my departure shortly after Labor Day. In a strange twist, she framed it as a retirement. She didn't consult me on this baffling shift in messaging. She surprised me with it on a Zoom call with my executive team colleagues, our faces arranged in boxes like the '70s television game show *The Hollywood Squares*. She was compelling in her delivery—believable, even—leaving me in the awkward position of smiling and nodding along. It was maddening. And exhausting. And dizzying, to watch my own story rewritten in real time.

As the days ticked by, I almost convinced myself it was a retirement. Ken and I were building a home in Maine, enabled by the equity I had earned from the company's sale. It was an investment, not a retirement home. I was too young to retire. More importantly, I wasn't done being a CPO. My return had been hard-won.

It seemed like my last day couldn't come fast enough.

And then, it did. December 15, 2020.

As I closed my laptop at the end of the day, I rested my head down on top of it. I didn't cry. I sat there wondering, *Now what?* A question I had repeated countless times in the last decade. Each time it felt different, yet also achingly similar.

Rolf Gates often says, "The pose begins when you want to leave it."

I planned to sit in the discomfort of this transition for a while. I'd learned through yoga, from Rolf, that the discomfort is the practice. Clarity doesn't come from moving quickly through unease, but from staying in.

Clarity comes from sitting still long enough to let the unknown show you what you're not ready to see—but need to. I reminded myself not to rush my next career move, as this one would surely be my last one before I left corporate life.

Yet, 2021 was barely underway when I received a call from a high-profile biology company, looking for a seasoned CPO to help them go public. I was flattered by their outreach but that wasn't what drew me to the opportunity. It was my ego, the part of me that had something to prove.

It wasn't redemption. It was defiance. Not the kind of grace I had worked so hard to practice, but a shallow middle finger to the company that had let me go. It felt sharp in the moment, but hollow almost as soon as I said, "Yes."

I didn't take that job to make a difference. I took it to prove something; I wasn't done. I wasn't retiring. I wanted to stay in the C-suite. And I wasn't leaving until I was ready to go. In Erikson's terms, midlife is a crossroads between generativity and stagnation—between growth that reaches outward or a retreat inward toward inertia.[42] In that moment, my choice leaned toward stagnation, fueled less by purpose than by a stubborn need to defend an identity I wasn't yet ready to release.

Just as my intuition from that long-ago day on the train told me my last job was the one, the place I belonged, I knew this job

---

[42] Erikson, *Identity: Youth and Crisis.*

was not that. And it didn't matter. It was as if all the wisdom I had spent years accumulating vanished in an instant.

Wisdom gave way to the longing of my inner nine-year-old, trying to matter, to be seen, to earn attention that should have been mine unconditionally. That little girl wasn't chasing a C-suite title, but the feeling was the same. Recognition. Relevance. Proof that I mattered. I knew better. I ignored the familiar echo of that longing, and my inner wisdom with it. I accepted the offer and agreed to start shortly thereafter.

It wasn't a disaster, but there was never any ease in the role. No flow. No rhythm. No belonging. Like trying to fit a square peg in a round hole. The work was familiar, but the context was entirely different. This company wasn't focused on culture or people. It was about winning. Dominance. Profit.

Those conditions didn't support the kind of generativity that had come to define how I now saw my role—as a leader who nurtures growth, fosters meaning, and shapes legacy. I'd slipped out of purpose and back into performance.

This wasn't like the other identity fractures I had experienced. Those came from external ruptures. This one was self-inflicted. I couldn't blame menopause, or the fire, or anything else. I had bypassed discomfort and chosen ego. Ancient yogis often say pain is inevitable, suffering optional. I chose suffering.

Only later did I recognize where I had landed developmentally. Generativity is the drive to create and nurture for the sake of future generations. Its shadow side is stagnation. A disconnection from purpose, a turning inward, a sense of futility.[43] That's where

---

[43] Erikson, *Identity: Youth and Crisis.*

I had landed. I had spiraled down, not up. The reality of this was painful.

Outwardly, it looked like I was a winner. On paper, it was a fantastic job. Prestige. Rewards. Potential. But stagnation is deceiving. It can appear like success superficially, but inwardly, it was draining, devouring my energy and spirit.

I had to find my way out of this conundrum I had created for myself.

On the bright side, if there was one, I had mastered the skill set of being a CPO. I could do the job. That wasn't the problem. It was the void in which I was doing it that created the emptiness and disillusionment. I started imagining my exit strategy within days of first stepping foot into the office.

I knew staying was not good for me. I had regressed. Staying might exacerbate it. I needed this misalignment to be a teacher, not an anchor.

I focused on what I had been hired to do. I would build the HR team, create the operating systems, and lay the foundation for the company to go public and grow. I wasn't going to let my poor decision sabotage my commitment or my integrity.

I did it with precision, not passion. There were no lighthearted moments with my boss in front of the whiteboard, no chats by the coffee machine with my colleagues, no emphasis on doing the right thing. It was a lonely, draining slog. One day, I arrived at the office early—it was still dark out—and as I turned the lights on and walked to my desk, I thought about the 5 a.m. runs I used to do when I trained for a marathon many years earlier. Even as I tied my sneakers and headed into the cold, dark morning, I was wishing the run was over. At least those runs ended. This seemed like it never would.

It took nearly a year to fulfill what I had promised to deliver when accepting this role, and as my one-year anniversary in the job approached, my internal dissonance was overwhelming. I worried it would surpass my ability to deliver. I needed an exit plan. I had to tell my boss. She was one of the founders, serious and driven, sometimes illogical despite her brilliance. We had a good rapport. I liked and respected her, which was more than I could say for many of my other colleagues.

In our weekly meeting, I shared the truth. This place wasn't a good fit for me. She looked at me, smiled timidly, and nodded knowingly, as if she had been waiting for this day. Rather than trying to talk me out of it or flatter me with false platitudes, she simply thanked me for honoring my commitment.

We agreed I would help find my replacement and leave once they came on board. A graceful ending, and a step forward from stagnation. Or was it a step back to generativity? I guess both.

I left a few months later. It was not the success with which I had hoped to end my corporate career, but it was closure. I knew without hesitation that it was time to leave. My career as a chief people officer ended. I stepped back freely and forward wholly. I let go. But this time, I sat in the discomfort, breathed into it, and let it reveal what I needed to learn.

I gave myself space, a self-imposed one-year time-out. I filled my time with yoga, trips to the library, long walks, and rest, lots of rest. We moved full-time to Maine. Other than one year in Portland previously, I had never lived anywhere but

Greater Boston. If my parents had still been alive, I probably would have hesitated. Their absence created a strange kind of freedom. And here, in Maine, we built a beautiful home, similar to our home before the fire. A reminder that even after loss, we can rebuild not just a house, but a sense of belonging.

Our home in Portland echoes with belonging. My sisters, my niece and nephews, and their growing families celebrate Thanksgiving here each year complete with board games, bowling, and trips to the local watering holes. It is a chaotic and fun weekend, reminiscent of the noisy, crowded holidays we had when my sisters and I were young. My in-laws and their delightful families come for Christmas, talking loudly over one another as Ken prepares a feast. And Alli and her longtime besties visit frequently to boat, drink wine, and share laughs by the fire pit. This house is finally home.

As Ken and I welcomed this new phase, Alli stepped fully into her own new chapter. She is grown now, her roots planted firmly in Massachusetts; she graduated college, earned a master's degree, and started her career in HR. She and her longtime boyfriend bought a house together. Her life is taking shape there, while mine has shifted in new directions.

At the end of my one-year time-out, I began writing, something I wanted to do since completing my dissertation. Writing emerged from the stillness, as did my story, my truth, and a desire to help others make sense of identity: its complexity and its brilliance. I found my voice. I became an advocate, speaking passionately about menopause in the workplace.

Another beginning. A true one. A gift. A privilege.

Every rupture, every letting go, had been its own practice. This time, I knew enough to stay in the pose. As Rolf Gates writes, "We show up, burn brightly in the moment, live passionately, and when the moment is over and our work is done, we step back and let go."[44]

---

[44] Rolf Gates and Katrina Kenison, *Meditations from the Mat: Daily Reflections on the Path of Yoga* (Vintage, 2002), 417.

Chapter 8

Theory Is Beautiful

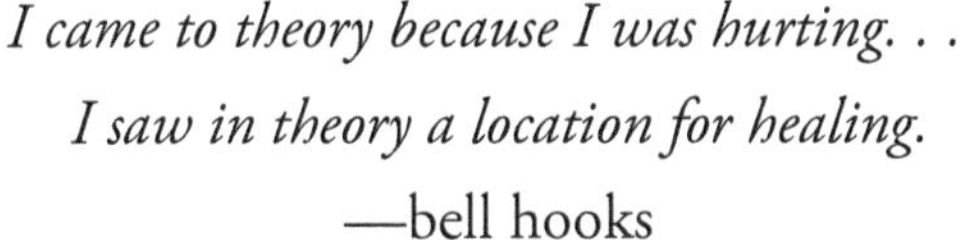

I came to theory because I was hurting. . . .
I saw in theory a location for healing.
—bell hooks

I met Dori on the first day of our PhD program in September 2011. We became fast friends and spent countless hours together in the early days of the program as we slogged through the grueling core courses required to even be considered for a doctoral degree. She was a natural academic, while I wasn't entirely sure what I was doing in a PhD program.

Sitting in the warm sun on campus, Dori would often ask, "Isn't theory beautiful?" as we were knee-deep in textbooks and literature reviews discussing complex human development theory. I would look at her aghast, not answering, grimacing, nodding absently, while thinking that she must mean that rhetorically. *Beautiful? This isn't even in English.*

Until I enrolled at Fielding, education had been a means to an end for me; my undergraduate and graduate degrees were oriented toward achievement and career. There hadn't been much beauty in either of those journeys. But my time at Fielding was different. At Fielding, it was not merely about getting a degree; it was about becoming a PhD. The doctoral path is not just academic. It is transformative. It reshapes how you think, how you make meaning, and how you see yourself in relation to the world.

My PhD studies became integral to rewriting my identity story, not just through scholarship but through the act of inquiry itself. My research became self-reflection as I explored the connection between friendship and self-esteem in adolescent girls, a tribute to my own developmental story.

Did I think theory was beautiful? No. Not really. At that point, I didn't even understand what Dori was talking about. But now—now, I do. Over time, theory became less confounding and more comforting. Theory offered me a framework for understanding my experiences and, ultimately, became part of my healing.

Theory provides a lens through which we can all see ourselves differently—more fully, more human. It opens possibilities—not just intellectually, but emotionally. It gives shape to the messiness of being human and helps us make sense of things that don't make sense.

You may be beginning to glimpse the possible beauty of theory. If not yet, I hope you might by the end of this chapter.

In sharing more theoretical depth here, my goal is to move beyond my own story and into the theoretical frameworks that shaped this book. Frameworks that invite you—the reader—to reflect on your own journey of becoming. I've engaged with many theories throughout the book, but here I focus on the ones that most shaped my understanding of self and identity.

Among all of the frameworks I encountered, *identity* emerged as the central lens—the perspective through which I came to understand both my story and myself. At the heart of any exploration of identity are three questions: Who am I? How did I get here? And where am I going? These are not merely personal inquiries; they are the foundation of identity theory as proposed by psychoanalyst Erik Erikson more than seventy-five years ago.[45]

Erikson positioned identity as the central organizing element of human development. It is what gives us a sense of direction and purpose. It is multifaceted and dynamic, a continual integration of past, present, and imagined future selves. Identity is not a singular fixed truth, but a layered and evolving process. It is continually changing as life unfolds.

Erikson's theory invites us to explore identity through multiple lenses: the ego lens, the personal lens, and the social lens. While interconnected, each is distinct and plays a role in his psychosocial model of development—the framework for which he is perhaps best known. *Ego identity* is our inner identity. Our internalized sense of self is collectively comprised of our values, beliefs, and goals. Ego identity provides the context in which our personal identity is formed and expressed. *Personal identity* is how our inner self is expressed in the world, through choices, pivotal moments, relationships, and life experiences. It is external and differentiating, reflecting the unique way we each show up and move through the world. *Social identity* is shaped by the roles we play and the groups we belong to, how we see ourselves in relation to others, and how they see us in return—each view shifting our

---

[45] Erikson, *Identity: Youth and Crisis.*

sense of self.[46] Together, these dimensions—ego, personal, and social—form a kind of three-way mirror, each angle influencing and reflecting the others.

Often, identity is thought of as fixed—something that once in place, remains there firmly. Yet I've come to understand, not only through Erikson's work but by living it, that identity reformulates throughout our lives. It is something we can shape through our choices, the chances we take, and our willingness to grow.

Erikson's psychosocial model of development outlines eight stages that unfold across the lifespan. Each stage poses a central tension: an internal question about who we are, what we value, and how we relate to the world around us. These tensions aren't meant to be perfectly resolved but to be engaged with, reflected on, and integrated.

When navigated with awareness and support, we are able to carry forward a foundational psychological strength to each stage: trust, autonomy, purpose, competence, authenticity, connection, care, and wisdom. These stages often correspond with age and are the building blocks of a coherent self. When one or more of these are disrupted or break down, our sense of self may falter. This is often thought of as an identity crisis or rupture, but reframed, it can be a chance to reformulate, or an opportunity to generate, not stagnate.

Like many, my internalized sense of self, my ego identity, evolved in what Erikson and other identity theorists would describe as a fairly typical trajectory. By early adolescence, it felt

---

[46] Kate C. McLean and Moin Syed, *The Oxford Handbook of Identity Development* (Oxford University Press, 2014), 3–4.

solid, dependable. I was competent, responsible, and oriented toward achievement. My personal identity crystallized around being the good student and dependable daughter. My social identity was anchored in friendships and community. The three strands—ego, personal, and social—were coherent and mutually reinforcing, which created an internal sense of resilience that felt almost unshakable.

Psychologists describe identity as inherently relational. We do not build it alone or in a vacuum. It is shaped in and through our closest connections.[47] Who we are is often reflected back not just by groups, but by the people we love, depend on, or struggle against. Family, friends, mentors, and partners hold up mirrors that affirm or challenge who we believe ourselves to be. Looking back, I can see how myriad relationships reflected versions of me that emphasized strength, capability, and self-reliance. Those reflections became part of my internal story of who I was.

For years, this tripartite identity served me well. It helped me recover quickly from missteps in my twenties and early thirties, and from the outside my life looked steady, even charmed. Only later would I understand how tightly woven these strands had become—and how vulnerable that coherence would be when confronted with rupture.

It wasn't until I was forty-two that I encountered such a rupture, an identity event that I didn't have the strength to withstand. The severe, unrecognized symptoms of menopause destabilized the internal coherence I had long relied on. What had

[47] Jordan, "Relational–Cultural Theory: The Power of Connection to Transform Our Lives."

once been a tightly integrated sense of self—ego, personal, and social identity working in harmony—began to fracture under the physiological strain.

It wasn't merely burnout or a midlife crisis; it was the dismantling of the self I had spent my life building. My professional identity had become so tightly fused with my ego, personal, and social identities that when I could no longer perform, the scaffolding gave way. In Erikson's terms, the strengths I had developed across earlier stages–competence, purpose, and autonomy—were suddenly inaccessible to me. The coherence that had guided me for decades disappeared into a blur almost overnight.

This collapse also revealed something I did not understand about my identity or identity more broadly. It had never been constructed solely from within. Much of my identity had been shaped in relation to how others saw me—or how I imagined they did. The sociologist Charles Horton Cooley describes this as the looking-glass self—the idea that we form our sense of who we are by imagining how others see us. Identity, then, isn't created in isolation, but shaped in relation to the social world around us.[48] For most of my life, I saw competence, strength, and success reflected back at me—not as an option, but as an imperative, my only chance at belonging. And so, that's who I became.

But when I could no longer perform in ways my identity demanded—the mirror shattered. The narrative dissolved, leaving me without coherence or direction. And then within a year, the fire compounded the rupture. My identity went from unstable

[48] Cooley, *Human Nature Social Order.*

to fully dismantled—a severing of continuity between my past, present, and imagined future.

In identity theory, this kind of collapse represents a breakdown of the narrative structure that weaves experience into a coherent sense of self over time, creating the liminal space in which an old identity has ended but a new one has not yet taken shape. Understanding what comes next requires a different lens—one that explains how we make (and remake) meaning when our story can no longer hold.

Dan P. McAdams's *narrative identity theory* weaves together Erikson's core questions—Who am I? How did I get here? Where am I going?—into an integrated life story approach to identity. It invites us to explore how our past, present, and imagined future selves connect to create meaning and consistency over time.[49]

Our narrative identity emerges from storytelling: the stories we tell ourselves, the ones we inherit, and the ones we come to accept as our own. These stories become part of how we understand who we are and—importantly—where we are going. Narrative identity doesn't differentiate ego, personal, and social identities. Instead, it sees them as an amalgamation, shaped and reshaped by key life experiences.

As McAdams often says, "We come to live in the story as we write it."

Storytelling shapes our sense of self, incorporating our hopes, goals, fears, and turning points. As humans, we strive for our stories to be intelligible—to make sense over time. When we encounter disruption—a bump in the road, or in my case, a land

---

[49] McAdams, *Power, Intimacy, Life Story.*

mine—we instinctively seek to restore our narrative, to reestablish equilibrium.

McAdams calls this process a redemptive narrative and sees it as essential to well-being, resilience, and generativity. Those who can integrate adversity into their life stories—not just to survive, but to grow—can evolve beyond the original plotline. They don't just move on. They rewrite the meaning of what came before.

From this perspective, the importance of storytelling in identity becomes unmistakable. Some identity ruptures are so profound that they don't simply disrupt the story—they fracture it entirely; imagining a new narrative feels impossible when the old one has collapsed. When everything familiar is gone, we must first find our footing, accept the loss, and acknowledge the disorientation before we can begin again. My own experience reflected this kind of disorientation, presenting as cognitive fog, emotional numbness, and a despair that made functioning nearly impossible.

Bessel van der Kolk, a leading expert on how the body stores trauma, describes this as a physical shutting down—a dissociation from consciousness in response to the overwhelming psychological assault of trauma. Trauma literally reshapes the brain, affecting the amygdala, prefrontal cortex, and hippocampus. Anxiety, fear, and reactive vigilance increase, while the ability to process information and retain memory decreases.[50]

For me, these symptoms were intensified by the havoc that menopause was wreaking on my brain. More broadly, for most women, estrogen, often called the brain's master regulator, plummets during menopause, affecting energy, memory, mood,

[50] van der Kolk, *Body Keeps the Score.*

and cognition. Dr. Lisa Mosconi refers to this constellation of symptoms as the *menopause brain*—and this misfiring played a central role in my decision to resign.[51]

And that was only my brain. The tentacles of menopause reach far beyond the brain to every place in the body where estrogen receptors reside—bones, liver, colon, skin, and salivary glands among them. The effects are broader than cognition and reproduction, intersecting with physical health, emotional well-being, and societal expectations. Viewed through a biopsychosocial lens, the full scope of menopause's impact on identity in midlife becomes clearer. It is a whole-person experience, touching body, mind, and place in society.[52]

Together, these biological, psychological, and social forces collided to further destabilize the core of my identity. The impact was devastating. It thrust me quickly into this nowhere space—a threshold between who I had been and who I might become. Anthropologists call this liminality, a state of uncertainty and possibility, a space where identity is no longer fixed but not yet re-formed.[53]

It sounds abstract, even esoteric, but liminality is fundamentally human. It's how we—across cultures and lifespans—move through change. It is the experience of in-betweenness itself, the difficulty in finding footing in uncertainty, and the quiet transformation that occurs in the process.

---

[51] Mosconi, *The Menopause Brain.*

[52] Kroger, *Identity Development: Adolescence Adulthood.*

[53] Nic Beech, "Liminality and the Practices of Identity Reconstruction," *Human Relations* 64, no. 2 (2011): 285–302; Bjørn Thomassen, "Thinking with Liminality" in *Breaking Boundaries: Varieties of Liminality*, ed. Agnes Horvath, Bjørn Thomassen, and Harald Wydra (Berghahn, 2015), 39–58.

There is no clarity in liminality, no guarantee of outcome. It can last a moment or years. To move forward, one must find a way to unstick themselves, write a new story, or free themselves from the in-between. Yoga became my way to navigate the chasm of liminality to find myself again.

The healing in stillness, the quiet beauty of yoga philosophy and the teachings of the Buddha were an unexpected gift. Where once I relied on action, striving, and muscling through, these teachings asked something unfamiliar of me: stillness, surrender, and trust.

While developmental theories offered frameworks for understanding identity, yoga provided a way to embody it. Under the guidance of my teacher, Rolf Gates, I began my healing with and through the *Yoga Sutras*.

Attributed to the sage Patanjali and believed to have been written between the 2nd century BCE and 4th century CE, the Sutras consist of 196 aphorisms, or sayings, that map the path of yoga as a way of being, not just a discipline.[54] It is impossible to distill them into a few key lessons, yet there are a few that I return to time and again. I'll share these and leave deeper exploration to those who find these adages as soothing and compelling as I do.

Perhaps most profoundly, yogic philosophy rests on a quiet but unwavering belief—we already have everything we need. The practice is not about becoming someone else; it's about leaving behind what no longer serves us, remembering that the present moment is the only one that matters, and recognizing that every day on the mat is a chance to begin again.

---

[54] Devi, *Secret Power of Yoga*.

The first Sutra (1.1) says it best: "With humility, an open heart, and a quiet mind, we begin the sacred study of yoga."[55] Yoga means union—it integrates physical, spiritual, and contemplative practices. It cultivates self-awareness, ethical behavior, and presence, while nurturing inner peace, focus, and well-being.

The eight-limb path, or Ashtanga, is perhaps the most well-known framework within the *Yoga Sutras.*[56] Since embracing it, it has become my comprehensive philosophical guide. A place I return to again and again. It grounded me when there seemed nothing left to return to, and it has remained with me even in later years, when the ruptures I faced were no longer land mines but simply bumps in the road.

I love the physical practice of yoga—the Asanas—but for the last two decades, my yoga practice has been much more. And Ashtanga is far more than a series of poses; it is a system, of which the poses are merely one step in the journey. The eight limbs—ethical precepts (Yama), self-discipline (Niyama), posture (Asana), breath regulation (Pranayama), sensory withdrawal (Pratyahara), concentration (Dharana), meditation (Dhyana), and union with the divine (Samadhi)—offer a progression toward deeper self-awareness and spiritual grounding.

I now embrace the deep interconnection of the eight limbs to identity. These teachings are not prescriptive steps but interwoven practices that invite reflection, intentionality, and presence. They offer a way to align inner and outer life, to examine what one is holding onto and what one might release. In this way, the

---

[55] Devi, *Secret Power of Yoga*, 12.

[56] Devi, *Secret Power of Yoga*, 173.

eight-limb path reflects a values-based model of identity—one that frees us from external definitions and supports the cultivation of the self from within.

Immersing myself in yoga meant exploring Buddhism. Much to my dismay, the average yoga studio often incorrectly implies that yoga lives within Buddhism. It does not, though the two share deep roots and complementary aims. In the larger spiritual context, both are paths of liberation, yoga through discipline and union, Buddhism through insight and compassion. They intersect around conscious practice, awareness, and transcendence of suffering.

Rolf's teachers frequently became my teachers, and he would often cite the work of Pema Chödrön, a Buddhist nun. Based on the title alone, I was drawn to one of her more well-known works *When Things Fall Apart.*[57] I hoped in the early days after the fire, often with a growing desperation, that there might be an answer inside her wisdom.

Unsurprisingly, there was not a tidy little list of what to do when things fall apart within the pages, but there was an invitation to stop striving, to stop waiting for the pain to end or the clarity to come. Pema writes, "The path is the goal." Therefore, healing, becoming, and reclaiming identity don't happen after rupture—they happen within it.

I am a natural fixer, a problem solver. Before my undoing, I had rarely met a challenge that I couldn't overcome. But here Chödrön was saying I didn't need to fix everything to be whole. I didn't need to rush toward resolution or restoration.

---

[57] Chodron, *When Things Fall Apart.*

Instead, I needed to learn to sit with discomfort, to witness the unknown, and to allow my identity to evolve through presence, not performance.

She wrote, "We think that the point is to pass the test or overcome the problem, but the truth is that things don't really get solved. They come together and they fall apart."

As I read this line over and over, I came to understand that my identity didn't need to be restored to its former shape. In fact, that was highly unlikely. My identity would come together and fall apart, again and again. What mattered was learning to stay present through each unfolding. What mattered was not holding on tighter to what had been but loosening my grip to make way for what could be.

This echoes Erikson's view that identity is not fixed but continually reformulated through crisis and change. What Pema frames as falling apart and coming together, Erikson describes as the lifelong rhythm of identity reconstruction.

Understanding identity as fluid and continually reformulated was not just a psychological insight. It was a spiritual one. The Sutras teach this through the fifth Yama—Aparigraha.[58] This Yama invites us to loosen our grip, not just on material possessions, but on identities, expectations, relationships, outcomes, and even beliefs. Aparigraha is about letting go of the need to control or cling, and instead, it is a lesson in cultivating trust in the unfolding of life.

This way of seeing myself—as fluid, evolving, unfinished—made space for something I was only beginning to understand.

---

[58] Devi, *Secret Power of Yoga*, 174.

There was no easy fix to my unraveling, no road back to who I was before the resignation, before the fire. I needed to release the confines of who I had been and allow these beautiful, ancient teachings to guide me forward. I had to trust the process, to let the path become the goal.

At the time, it didn't occur to me—nor did I have the energy—to explore the deeper origins of my identity. I wasn't yet ready to relook at the second important question underscoring identity: How did I get here? Healing the trauma consuming me required everything I had. It wasn't until I began writing this book that I turned to my childhood to more fully understand the roots of my identity story.

For me, the beauty of the theoretical framework of childhood emotional neglect (CEN) lies not in its academic rigor but in its deep personal resonance.[59] For the first time, I had language to describe my childhood trauma—trauma that had long felt unresolved, its nature imprecise, which made it difficult to articulate or trace its impact. When I came across the work of Dr. Jonice Webb and her colleagues, it was as if a light switched on. She didn't just describe an experience; she described me. My parents loved me—I know that. But they didn't *see* me. And the absence of that emotional attunement has been a quiet struggle I've carried throughout my life.

Although the research on CEN is still emerging and grounded more in clinical observation than large-scale empirical study, I include it here because it made visible why I had so long felt invisible. It illuminated something essential at the core of

---

[59] Webb, *Running on Empty.*

my identity. Understanding this helped me make sense of my past and offered a frame through which to tell this story.

Dr. Webb writes, "Childhood Emotional Neglect hides not in what did happen, but in what didn't happen." CEN is not overt abuse or cruelty—it is the absence of adequate emotional attunement. It stems from a parent's inability to recognize and respond to a child's emotional needs, leaving the child feeling as though they don't belong or aren't worthy of being seen.

In *Running on Empty*, Webb outlines a range of parenting styles that can lead to CEN and explores how they shape the inner lives of adult children. A common thread runs through these parenting styles. They are often loving, well-meaning parents whose emotionally neglectful behaviors appear subtle, even normal.

One example is the achievement or perfection-focused parent. When a child brings home mostly As and Bs, the parent ignores the overall accomplishment and instead highlights only the missing As. Another example is the well-intentioned parent who was emotionally neglected themselves. These parents often neglect a child's feelings because they were never taught that feelings matter. They may not understand that healthy development requires emotional connection, not just material support or discipline.

Webb outlines roughly a dozen parenting styles she describes as "mildly emotionally neglectful." While they vary, they share a few key traits: an absence of praise or encouragement, an overemphasis on self-sufficiency, and general emotional unavailability.

For children of CEN, the legacy often shows up in adulthood as chronic feelings of emptiness, a sense of never being quite good enough, difficulty accessing or expressing emotions, and a quiet belief that something is inherently wrong with them.

It is a subtle, visceral longing—one that often goes unrecognized for decades. Many adults with CEN learn to overcompensate, masking the loss of connection with self-reliance, achievement, and determination. From the outside, they appear strong; inside, they often feel unknown—even to themselves.

When I look back at my childhood, my memories of my parents are fond. I don't want to dishonor the love they had for me by critiquing their parenting too closely. Instead, I've found comfort in understanding that so much of who I became—driven, self-reliant, outwardly composed—makes sense through the lens of CEN.

This lens also helped me see why I had spent much of my life in my head, propelled by the constant voices telling me to do better, be better. It also explained why embodied healing was essential—not only for recovering from the identity disruption and trauma of my adult life, but for finding the courage to rewrite my story and connect with the parts of myself I had long ignored, or perhaps never truly knew. This search would take me through a shifting landscape of possible selves—versions of me I could barely imagine earlier in my life.

In retrospect, I see CEN as the backdrop to my long journey back to myself—a journey in which I meandered down many paths, exploring possible directions. I was no longer trying to reclaim my old self; I was searching for who I could become. At the time, it often felt frivolous or even irresponsible, but I now see it as necessary. For the first time, I was discovering a sense of self that was intrinsically motivated—rooted in my own needs and wants, no longer driven by approval or a desperate desire to belong.

With this perspective, my wandering now made sense. It had a name, a place in the psychology of identity, and even a framework to explain why I kept trying on new versions of myself. I was delighted to learn that this kind of exploration wasn't what was keeping me from returning to the C-suite, but rather it was expanding my options and was grounded in the foundational research on "possible selves" by Hazel Markus and Paula Nurius in their pioneering 1986 paper.[60]

Markus and Nurius describe possible selves as the visions we hold of who we might become, who we hope to become, and who we fear becoming. Their work demonstrates the link between self-concept and motivation and, in many ways, supports McAdams's narrative identity theory. Possible selves are the cognitive components of our hopes, fears, goals, and threats. They give meaning, organization, and direction to our lives, connecting the present self to motivation and behavior, and guiding us toward selves we wish to approach—or away from those we want to avoid. They also provide an evaluative lens, shaping how we interpret current experiences through imagined future possibilities.

This framework reinforces the understanding that identity is not monolithic or static, but fluid—a multiplicity of possibilities that shift with context, time, and social experience. Accessing possible selves can influence resilience, recovery, and personal growth after a crisis or failure. And like narrative identity, they highlight the social shaping of the self. In many ways, possible selves are the raw material from which narrative identity is constructed,

---

[60] Markus and Nurius, "Possible Selves."

offering the characters and plots we test, elaborate, and ultimately weave into our life story. Dan P. McAdams has written, "Selves create stories, which in turn create selves."[61]

I now deeply understand what Pema Chödrön meant when she said, "The path is the goal."[62] My journey had been, in many ways, an unwitting experiment in possible selves—testing who I might become, discarding what didn't fit, and slowly shaping a story that felt like my own.

Over time, my love for theory deepened into excitement at how rigorous academic research often echoes spiritual teachings in unexpected ways. Tedeschi and Calhoun's post-traumatic growth theory (PTG) mirrors the Buddhist insight that great good can emerge from great suffering. It is the wrestling with trauma—not the trauma itself—that fosters growth. Healing is not the reward for solving the trauma; it is born in the very act of grappling with it.[63]

Positive growth after trauma is rarely a conscious goal. In the wake of a death, assault, accident, or illness, simply putting one foot in front of the other can feel like the most we can manage. In the all-consuming work of creating a new normal, searching for meaning may seem unthinkable.

And yet, we often hear stories where tragedy becomes a turning point, a catalyst for transformation. These stories hold a before and an after, a rewriting of the self, a new life narrative. PTG links wisdom and narrative development, emerging when survivors balance reflection with action, weigh what is known against

---

[61] McAdams, "Narrative Identity."

[62] Chodron, *When Things Fall Apart.*

[63] Tedeschi and Calhoun, "The Posttraumatic Growth Inventory."

what is unknowable, accept life's paradoxes, and remain open to the fundamental questions of human existence.

Following a psychologically seismic event, survivors challenge their deepest assumptions, and begin to rebuild their story, integrating their trauma into a new framework for growth. This framework encompasses five domains: personal strengths, new possibilities, relating to others, spiritual change, and appreciation of life.

These domains are not linear. They often overlap and coexist with ongoing grief and distress. The growth that emerges is real and often profound, but it does not erase the devastation of the trauma. Transformation in this context is a fundamental change—an altered way of being in the world—born not from the trauma itself, but from the struggle to live with it. This kind of transformation reshapes how we understand power.

Power is not the same as powering through. Powering through is not about becoming invisible, accepting less, or pretending you are not broken. It is not about shame, resignation, or allowing others to define you. It is about sinking roots deeper—not in the shallow soil of others' expectations, but in the rich ground of everything you have endured, everyone who has loved you, and everything you have become. It is about claiming the right to grow strong from that ground—to be whole, to be seen, and to be valued.[64]

---

[64] Joanne Harris (@joannechocolat), "On Power, and on Powering Through, and Why They're Really Not the Same," Tumblr, accessed August 27, 2025, https://www.tumblr.com/joannechocolat/712309194622140416/on-power-and-on-powering-through-and-why-theyre.

Theory helped me see my journey more clearly. It was pivotal in recovering my agency and in stepping into a version of myself that felt whole. Whole in that moment, whole for that time. Because I've learned that wholeness—like identity—is never fixed.

Things come together, they fall apart, and they come together again—an endless rhythm we learn to live within.

Afterword

Becoming Again and Again

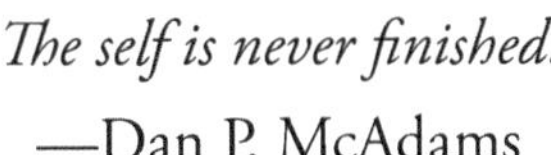

The self is never finished.
—Dan P. McAdams

This book began with rupture. My identity, once so solid and durable, crumbled under the weight of vague, undiagnosable symptoms. Symptoms without edges, yet powerful enough to shatter the life I had built. Nebulous forces with the strength to derail the career I had dedicated myself to for twenty years, unconvincing indicators substantial enough to undermine my marriage, and formless warnings able to devastate my health.

These debilitating signals, invisible to others yet undeniable to me, left me desperate enough to walk away rather than risk further destruction. Yet destruction came anyway. In the throes of my eventual menopause diagnosis, a second pillar of my identity collapsed when fire destroyed my home and everything in it just a year later.

Disruption doesn't seem sufficient to capture the magnitude of what had become a full-blown identity crisis. The very core of my being was no longer supported by the narrative that had scaffolded me for decades. At forty-two, I began to learn that identity is not a destination. It is not static. You don't get there and stay there, impervious to destruction. It is a rhythm of shattering and reassembling, of being undone and remade.

As I look back, I see that every ending carried within it a beginning I could not yet imagine. Time and again, I thought I was finished, rebuilt, complete—only to discover I was still unfolding. Wholeness, I now understand, is never permanent. It is provisional, a temporary integration that steadies us for what comes next—the next shift, the next unraveling, the next time things fall apart.

Within those fleeting moments of steadiness, I embraced the practices, stories, and theories that helped me heal—not in spite of the struggle but because of it. Yoga taught me the power of the pause, the breath between inaction and action, where clarity resides. Writing reminded me of what rupture tries to erase—bringing forward my story, my truth, and shedding light on essential pieces of my identity that had been too long left in the dark.

These are not anchors but touchstones—threads that connect who I have been, who I am now, and who I am still becoming. Integration, I've come to see, is less a single act than an ongoing rhythm: aligning with what is true in this moment, translating experience into meaning. It is the quiet work of digesting our stories and carrying them forward into daily life in ways that ripple outward—shaping our families, our communities, and our world.

As the ancient yogis say, it is the forever journey of bringing the unconscious to the conscious, the unseen to the seen, the unreal to the real. Through this weaving, across generations and across time, we remember our inherent interconnectedness, our place within the greater order of life, and the truth that all we seek already resides within us.

As I look back, I see that I have carried many selves across my life—the curious one, the brave one, the driven one, the one who broke open, the one who made meaning. They rose when I needed them the most, each offering something essential to my becoming.

And if this is true for me, I know it is also true for you. We all carry such selves. They rise and recede across a lifetime, guiding us, unsettling us, steadying us, and asking us to grow. They teach us who we have been—and who we are still becoming. Each self has something to teach, and each self matters. My hope is that you have found some part of yourself in these pages—a reflection, a reminder, or simply the reassurance that you are not alone.

If there is one truth this journey has taught me, it is that we are never fully knowable—not even to ourselves. We think we know someone, or even who we ourselves are, only to discover that identity is never fixed. It shifts and rearranges, it falls apart and comes together, it reveals layers we did not know existed. Every rupture carries within it a beginning not yet visible. Every ending makes space for what is still to be born.

The question is not whether change will come. It will. The invitation is how we will meet it—with curiosity, with courage, and, when we can, with grace.

We are never finished—only ever becoming, again and again.

References

Arnett, Jeffrey Jensen. "Emerging Adulthood: A Theory of Development from the Late Teens through the Twenties." *American Psychologist* 55, no. 5 (2000): 469.

American Academy of Arts and Sciences. "Attrition in Humanities Doctorate Programs." Accessed August 27, 2025. https://www.amacad.org/humanities-indicators/higher-education/attrition-humanities-doctorate-programs.

Barlow, David H. "Time to Reflect on the Women's Health Initiative (WHI) Study." *Human Reproduction* 18, no. 1 (2003).

Beech, Nic. "Liminality and the Practices of Identity Reconstruction." *Human Relations* 64, no. 2 (2011): 285–302.

Bowlby, John. "The Bowlby-Ainsworth Attachment Theory." *Behavioral and Brain Sciences* 2, no. 4 (1979): 637–38.

Chodron, Pema. *When Things Fall Apart: Heart Advice for Difficult Times*. Shambhala Publications, 2000.

Clance, Pauline Rose, and Maureen Ann O'Toole. "The Imposter Phenomenon: An Internal Barrier to Empowerment and Achievement." In *Women's Way of Knowing*, edited by Mary Field Belenky, Blythe McVicker Clinchy, Nancy Rule Goldberger, and Jill Mattuck Tarule. Basic Books, 1988.

Cooley, C. *Human Nature and the Social Order*. Scribner, 1902.

Devi, N. J. *The Secret Power of Yoga*. Harmony Books, 2022.

Duke, Marshall P., Amber Lazarus, and Robyn Fivush. "Knowledge of Family History as a Clinically Useful Index of Psychological Well-Being and Prognosis: A Brief Report." *Psychotherapy: Theory, Research, Practice, Training* 45, no. 2 (2008): 268.

Engel, G. "The Need for a New Medical Model: A Challenge for Biomedicine." *Science* 196, no. 4286 (1977): 129–36.

Erikson, E. *Identity: Youth and Crisis*. Norton, 1968.

Gates, Rolf, and Katrina Kenison. *Meditations from the Mat: Daily Reflections on the Path of Yoga*. Vintage, 2002.

Gopaldas, Ahir. "Intersectionality 101." *Journal of Public Policy & Marketing* 32 (2013): 90–94.

Greer, Germaine. *The Change: Women, Ageing and the Menopause*. Bloomsbury Publishing, 2018.

Hanh, Thich Nhat. *No Death, No Fear: Comforting Wisdom for Life*. Penguin, 2003.

Harris, Joanne. "On Power, and on Powering Through, and Why They're Really Not the Same." Tumblr, accessed August 27, 2025. https://www.tumblr.com/joannechocolat/712309194622140416/on-power-and-on-powering-through-and-why-theyre.

Harman, Laura. "73% of Women Say Menopause Was Key Factor in Their Divorce." Woman and Home, 2022. https://www.womanandhome.com/life/world-menopause-day-2022-study-reveals-73-of-women-believe-menopause-was-a-contributing-factor-in-their-divorce/.

Harter, Susan. *The Construction of the Self: Developmental and Sociocultural Foundations*. 2nd ed. The Guilford Press, 2012.

Hemphill, Prentis. *What It Takes to Heal: How Transforming Ourselves Can Change the World*. Random House, 2025.

Jordan, Judith V. "Relational–Cultural Theory: The Power of Connection to Transform Our Lives." *The Journal of Humanistic Counseling* 56, no. 3 (2017): 228–43.

Kroger, Jane. *Identity Development: Adolescence through Adulthood*. 2nd ed. Sage Publications, 2007.

Lock, Margaret. "The Politics of Mid-Life and Menopause." In *Knowledge, Power, and Practice: The Anthropology of Medicine in Everyday Life*, edited by Shirley Lindenbaum and Margaret Lock. University of California Press, 1993, 330–63.

Markus, Hazel, and Paula Nurius. "Possible Selves." *American Psychologist* 41, no. 9 (1986): 954.

McAdams, Dan P. "Narrative Identity: What Is It? What Does It Do? How Do You Measure It?" *Imagination, Cognition and Personality* 37, no. 3 (2018): 359–72. https://doi.org/10.1177/0276236618756704.

McAdams, Dan P. *Power, Intimacy, and the Life Story: Personological Inquiries into Identity*. Guilford Press, 1988.

McLean, Kate C., and Moin Syed. *The Oxford Handbook of Identity Development*. Oxford University Press, 2014.

Mishra, Gita D., Melanie C. Davies, Sarah Hillman, et al. "Optimising Health after Early Menopause." *The Lancet* 403, no. 10430 (2024): 958–68.

Mosconi, Lisa. *The Menopause Brain*. Penguin Random House, 2024.

Nappi, R., and K. Schaudig. "Perimenopause and Menopause: An Opportunity to Engage, Inform, and Empower Women to Live Well." *European Medical Journal* 8, no. 4 (2023): 47–53.

Northrup, Christiane. *The Wisdom of Menopause: Creating Physical and Emotional Health and Healing During the Change*. Bantam Books, 2001.

Salmon, Catherine, and Katrin Schumann. *The Secret Power of Middle Children: How Middleborns Can Harness Their Unexpected and Remarkable Abilities*. Penguin, 2012.

Shamir, Boas, Hava Dayan-Horesh, and Dalya Adler. "Leading by Biography: Towards a Life-Story Approach to the Study of Leadership." *Leadership* 1, no. 1 (2005): 13–29.

Stapleton, Andy. "How Many People Have PhDs? Number of People With Doctoral Degree." Academia Insider. August 27, 2024. https://academiainsider.com/how-many-people-have-phds/.

Tedeschi, Richard G., and Lawrence G. Calhoun. "The Post-traumatic Growth Inventory: Measuring the Positive Legacy of Trauma." *Journal of Traumatic Stress* 9 (n.d.): 455–71.

Tedeschi, Richard G., and Lawrence G. Calhoun. "Posttraumatic Growth: Conceptual Foundations and Empirical Evidence." *Psychological Inquiry* 15, no. 1 (2004): 1–18.

Thomassen, Bjørn. "Thinking with Liminality." *Breaking Boundaries: Varieties of Liminality*, Berghahn, 2015, 39–58.

Ussher, Jane M., and Jane Ussher. *The Madness of Women: Myth and Experience*. Routledge, 2011.

van der Kolk, B. *The Body Keeps the Score: Brain, Mind, and Body in the Healing of Trauma*. Viking, 2014.

Webb, Jonice. *Running on Empty: Overcome Your Childhood Emotional Neglect*. Morgan James Publishing, 2012.

Acknowledgments

My deepest thanks go to the people who helped bring this book—and me—into being.

My husband, Ken, has met every unraveling and reimagining with love that is steady, imperfect, and enduring. You have been the ground beneath my becoming, the place I rebuild from again and again. And my daughter, Allison—thank you for teaching me to soften, to let go, and simply to be. You have been my most honest mirror, one that made me better. Being your mother is my greatest privilege.

My colleagues have shaped me in ways that shine through every chapter of this book. You inspired me to lead with more integrity, purpose, and curiosity than I knew I had. You challenged me to be better and believed in me with a generosity that made me brave. Your faith in me means everything.

My friends, lifelong and recent, encouraged me to write, boosting my confidence at moments when mine wavered. You laughed with me, cried with me, and held me close, giving me the strength to keep going.

My mentors and teachers showed me wisdom, humility, and grace. You expanded my understanding of what leadership and humanity could be and encouraged me in moments when I doubted myself. You helped ground me when I lost my way.

My family—my nieces and nephews, my sisters, my parents, my in-laws, my cousins, and the aunts and uncles who shaped me—thank you for being both roots and branches. You remind me where I come from and how far I can reach.

I am also grateful for the early readers, trusted confidants, and fellow seekers who engaged with these pages long before they were ready for the world. Your reflections, questions, and encouragement helped ensure my story carried both truth and heart.

And to the editors, designers, and professionals who helped bring this manuscript to life—your care and thoughtfulness are woven into every chapter.

Thank you for walking this path with me. Your encouragement helped transform this story into a book.

With love and gratitude,
Susan

About the Author

Susan A. Miele is a writer, scholar, and former Chief People Officer whose work explores how identity is dismantled and redefined through life's transitions. Drawing from her own experience and her PhD in Human and Organizational Systems, she writes at the intersection of personal transformation, theory, and leadership, challenging how we think about belonging, success, and change.

A lifelong learner and dedicated yogi, Susan infuses her writing and speaking with mindfulness and compassion. Her work invites readers and organizations alike to see disruption not as loss, but as a profound opportunity for growth. She lives in Portland, Maine.

Continue the Conversation

If this book resonated with you, I'd love to stay connected. You can find more of my writing, resources, and reflections on identity, transitions, and becoming at susanmiele.com.

You can also subscribe to my monthly newsletter on Substack at susanannmiele.substack.com, where I share essays, stories, and thoughts on navigating life's many seasons.

The B Corp Movement

Dear reader,

Thank you for reading this book and joining the Publish Your Purpose community! You are joining a special group of people who aim to make the world a better place.

What's Publish Your Purpose About?

Our mission is to elevate the voices often excluded from traditional publishing. We intentionally seek out authors and storytellers with diverse backgrounds, life experiences, and unique perspectives to publish books that will make an impact in the world.

Beyond our books, we are focused on tangible, action-based change. As a woman- and LGBTQ+-owned company, we are committed to reducing inequality, lowering levels of poverty, creating a healthier environment, building stronger communities, and creating high-quality jobs with dignity and purpose.

As a Certified B Corporation, we use business as a force for good. We join a community of mission-driven companies building a more equitable, inclusive, and sustainable global economy. B Corporations must meet high standards of transparency, social and environmental performance, and accountability as determined by the nonprofit B Lab. The certification process is rigorous and ongoing (with a recertification requirement every three years).

How Do We Do This?

We intentionally partner with socially and economically disadvantaged businesses that meet our sustainability goals. We embrace and encourage our authors and employee's differences in race, age, color, disability, ethnicity, family or marital status, gender identity or expression, language, national origin, physical and mental ability, political affiliation, religion, sexual orientation, socio-economic status, veteran status, and other characteristics that make them unique.

Community is at the heart of everything we do—from our writing and publishing programs to contributing to social enterprise nonprofits like reSET (https://www.resetco.org/) and our work in founding B Local Connecticut.

We are endlessly grateful to our authors, readers, and local community for being the driving force behind the equitable and sustainable world we are building together.

To connect with us online, or publish with us,
visit us at www.publishyourpurpose.com.

Elevating Your Voice,

Jenn T Grace

Jenn T. Grace

Founder, Publish Your Purpose

www.ingramcontent.com/pod-product-compliance
Ingram Content Group UK Ltd.
Pitfield, Milton Keynes, MK11 3LW, UK
UKHW062311290726
14090UKWH00018B/998

9 798887 972336